Radical Hospitality: Benedict's Way of Love

2017 Fourth Printing New and Expanded Edition
2016 Third Printing New and Expanded Edition
2014 Second Printing New and Expanded Edition
2011 First Printing New and Expanded Edition
2002 First Printing Original Edition

ISBN: 978-1-55725-891-5

Excerpts from the Rule of St. Benedict are taken from *The Rule of St. Benedict in Latin and English with Notes* (Collegeville, MN: Liturgical Press, 1981).

The Paraclete Press name and logo (dove and cross) are trademarks of Paraclete Press, Inc.

Library of Congress Cataloging–in–Publication Data
Pratt, Lonni Collins, 1953-
    Radical hospitality : Benedict's way of love / Lonni Collins Pratt with Daniel Homan.—New expanded ed.
        p. cm.
    Rev. ed. of: Benedict's way.
    ISBN 978-1-55725-891-5
1. Benedictines—Spiritual life. 2. Hospitality—Religious aspects—Christianity.
I. Homan, Daniel, O.S.B. II. Pratt, Lonni Collins, 1953- Benedict's way. III.
Title.
    BX3003.P73 2011
    241'.671—dc22   2011006326

10 9 8 7 6 5 4

Published by Paraclete Press
Brewster, Massachusetts
www.paracletepress.com
Printed in the United States of America

radical

hospitality

— NEW & EXPANDED EDITION —

radical *hospitality* ™

benedict's way of love

LONNI COLLINS PRATT WITH **FATHER DANIEL HOMAN,** OSB

PARACLETE PRESS
BREWSTER, MASSACHUSETTS

"All guests who present themselves are to be welcomed as Christ, for he himself will say: 'I was a stranger and you welcomed me.'"

—*The Rule of St. Benedict* 53:1

"Once a guest has been announced, the superior and the community are to meet the guest with all the courtesy of love."

—*The Rule of St. Benedict* 53:3

"Great care and concern are to be shown in receiving poor people and pilgrims, because in them more particularly Christ is received."

—*The Rule of St. Benedict* 53:15

"Let us open our eyes to the deifying light, let us hear with attentive ears the warning which the divine voice cries daily to us, 'Today if you hear his voice, harden not your hearts.'"

—*The Rule of St. Benedict*, Prologue 29

contents

New Introduction

"If we take seriously the call to radical hospitality, we will discover the true meaning of ministry," the pastor said to his congregation. It was Sunday morning in Dayton. "The birth of the radical hospitality movement in our congregation can be traced to one guy reading a book a few years ago. This isn't some new spiritual fad, though. We have been awakened to our indifference by the Holy Spirit, and in the process of learning to welcome and care for those who are unlike us, we are on the gospel road. I know, I know, it sounds like a song our grandparents might have sung at camp-meeting doesn't it?"

Hospitality is at the heart of Christianity. No one has ever been more radically welcoming than Jesus, who was always accused of associating with the wrong kind of people—people we wouldn't want in our living rooms, or next to us worshiping.

The phrase *radical hospitality* refers to the activities and desires that inspire individuals and communities to welcome those who are unlike themselves. Rather than viewing any person in terms of how they benefit us, radical hospitality means accepting the person with no thought of personal benefit. Instead of seeking persons who will support the congregation, actively seek persons who need the support of the congregation. To become hospitable means finding ways to welcome the marginalized, forgotten, and misunderstood among us.

Our world feels no safer than it did when the first edition of this book, *Radical Hospitality*, was originally published. Back then, we were still staggering after September 11, 2001. The falling towers were still in our minds. Fear and an awareness of our vulnerability had taken up residence.

In addition to our fears, we have become a culture with more disdain and indifference than before. Today, human kindness often seems under siege. In the midst of this, some of us are looking for ways to grow more hospitable. Regardless of where our search may take us, it must begin, for all, with a turning inside and ruthless self-evaluation. An examination of conscience that scorches away the excuses we grant ourselves is not just needed; our lives and our society may depend upon it.

For example, it is our nature to seek out persons who are like us for mutual support and affirmation. And it is typical of religious groups to reach out to persons who have something to bring to their congregation, a contribution to make. Most often when you join a church you're asked to pledge your abilities, time, and resources to support the faith community. As a church, we have become accustomed to viewing our membership in terms of what others can give the local congregation. We actively seek out productive, contributing members of our community.

But radical hospitality calls us to search for the lost ones, those who have nothing to give us, but who, instead, need something from us. They may or may not be aware of what they have to give in return. Radical hospitality does not keep a ledger of what is given and what is received.

Certainly there are faith communities that are better at radical hospitality than most. In Detroit, Cass Community United Methodist Church is just such an example. The Reverend Faith Fowler is the pastor, and she has brought a new day to this battered place.

Having grown up in the Detroit area, I have long heard stories of the Cass Corridor, one of the nation's most impoverished regions. Cass Avenue is where Faith and her congregation are located. Think of the toughest inner-city district you know. Home to drug-dealing, crime, and prostitution. A place where the homeless are propped against walls of vacant buildings after they've been brutally beaten and robbed of half a bottle of cheap wine. A dumping ground for those with addictions and mental illness. A place avoided by nice church people. Faith and her congregation call that place home.

A few years ago, Faith came to Heritage United Methodist Church, the congregation where my husband, David, is pastor, in rural Michigan. The two churches are as different as two congregations can be. Faith told us stories from her life. She's been robbed so many times she's lost count. Our church has been broken into, but the culprits used oversized cabbages to break a window—there were no guns or knives. We have a few families who have members with special needs. Faith's entire congregation would be labeled "special needs" by our group.

When Faith spoke of what they are doing in Detroit to strengthen and grow a community of faith that will support and serve the needs of those who live in and around the Cass Corridor, she never mentioned the phrase *radical hospitality*—but Faith has lived it and she has led the people she serves into the very depths of radical hospitality. The Cass Community Church is bringing hope to a place where once the warning, "Abandon hope all ye who enter here," was fitting.

Of course, most of us don't live in places like Detroit's Cass Corridor. The outcasts among us are not quite so obvious.

Not too long ago, I was watching an episode of the *Andy Griffith Show* with my granddaughter Gina. Gina is thirteen and she adores Mayberry. She is not old enough to have seen the original classic television show starring Andy Griffith as the wise and cheerful sheriff of a little southern town named Mayberry, but the show exists in reruns and on DVDs. Gina has enthusiastically discovered both.

The particular episode we happened to watch together was about Sheriff Andy, Deputy Barney, and a troop of boys going into the woods on a rustic camping trip. Barney is, of course, making a lot of noise about how he knows the wilderness, can live off the land, and never gets lost, blah, blah, blah. Predictably,

Barney and some of the boys, when they are off on their own, become lost.

The boys say, "Hey, Deputy Fife, we'll be okay because you can catch our dinner and start a fire." Barney would be challenged to start a fire with straw and matches. But, there he is, trapped in his big-man talk, about to look like a fool to a group of small boys. Except, he has one thing going for him—he has the best friend of all time—Andy.

When the little group doesn't return, Andy goes searching and finds them, but doesn't reveal himself right away. Remaining hidden, he figures out Barney has gotten himself into a heap of trouble, so while no one is looking, Sheriff Andy starts the cooking fire and places over it the roasted chicken Aunt Bea sent out for his dinner. Barney ends up a hero.

When the show finished, Gina looked at me, clearly baffled. She said, "The boys never know that Barney was bragging? That he didn't know what he was talking about?"

I shook my head, "They never know."

"It would be funny. He made a fool of himself. They could all laugh at him. They'd learn not to act that way."

"Which, you know, is how it would go on the Disney channel," I said. "It would be another chance to laugh at the little awkward guy who tries too hard."

"It. Would. Be. Funny." She replied slowly and clearly.

Don't we all wish for a friend who will cover our self-delusional silliness? Sometimes it seems that we've moved so far from such an idea that the notion of a friend like Sheriff Andy is just . . . foreign. These days, we often pull away and let people sink. We call it tough love to leave people choking on their mistakes. Why do we do that?

How do you press against darkness? How do you remain or become an agent of change or transformation? Every now and then a good reason to strive for countercultural comes along—this is one of those times.

Radical hospitality must uncompromisingly remain fundamental to its revolutionary nature. This is not to say that the word *radical* necessarily means "extremist"—it doesn't. *Radical* refers to what is fundamental, or the root of something. You may remember from high school science that the term *radical* also describes an atom that doesn't lose its identity during change. Our identity as people of faith and communities of faith will be gained, not lost, in the changes required to become radically hospitable.

Hospitality that is radical is needed now more than ever before. This is obvious when you drive, shop, eat at a restaurant, or send a child to school. I've read reports of bus drivers yelling at their passengers because they're too slow getting seated or their toddler wets a seat. One day I sat in the office of the local middle school and heard a girl walk up behind a boy and say, "You're such a fag. Did they finally throw you out of school?" Maybe I see more of this disdain than a lot of other people do because I hang out in a middle school and with teens, but, an attitude of contempt is not limited to young people.

Jesus had a radical idea. He said love the ones who are hard to love, love your "enemy." I don't know about you, but I can't really think of anyone who qualifies as my enemy. However, this disdain I've mentioned is an enemy that threatens the way we all relate to each other. If I'm not vigilant about it, I just may find that some of this contempt has ebbed into my own way of thinking and viewing others. I sense my own hard edges and sometimes hear myself chinking against others.

Hospitality has not become easier since the original version of this book. The world has not become an easier place to live, and our lives together only grow increasingly complicated. Annie Dillard once wrote, "The way we spend our days is the way we spend our lives." The way I spend my days—there's a place to start.

To intentionally live counterculturally is not for the timid. Radical hospitality has not only a spiritual but a social and economic impact. Radical hospitality is not about being what one monk called "Minnesota nice" (referring to how really polite Minnesotans are); it is about transforming our hearts and our communities. It is about justice for every soul.

Hospitality as it has been expressed and lived within monasticism is a strong example to follow—but it isn't the only way to live a hospitable life. The lessons we learn from monks are examples for us, but we confront the issues of hospitality in the realms of our own lives, most of which are not lived in monasteries.

My grandmother once told me that most people won't care one way or another about me. She didn't want to take a swipe at my self-esteem when she uttered the words I've never forgotten. She was trying to make the point that my family loves me and most other people don't. These people who love me also influence me, but I have learned through the years that I can influence them as well. It's right here in my own circle of friends, family, neighbors, and coworkers that I most recognize my power for good and my ability to exercise that power.

One of the peculiarities about really hospitable people is that they don't go out looking for ways to be hospitable; they simply give it a try when there's a chance to do so. It isn't about results, it's about changing the universe by becoming available to one person in one sliver of time.

I knew a guy who was convinced that the new neighbor in his condo complex was out to find a husband and had set her cap for him. She had sent him a Christmas card, left a plate of cookies on his porch, and returned his dog when it had gotten away. He told several people about the "desperate attempts" she had made to get his attention. His words got back to her. Over lunch one day, he told me that she pounded on his door and when he opened it, she said that next time she'd call someone to pick up his dog if it got loose.

Through tears she said, "You could have given me a chance to just be your neighbor. Have you never had a neighbor before?"

There's a person in Scripture who asks Jesus, "Who is my neighbor?" The person asking the question wanted to be sure he got it right, in a legalistic sense. We get the impression that the questioner is concerned with doing the minimum expected from him by the law. Plus, what might be the consequences of being neighborly to someone who isn't actually a neighbor? It would have been helpful had Jesus set up terms and limitations to clarify what constitutes a neighbor. Instead Jesus told the story of the Good Samaritan, and in the story we learn that our neighbor is found in the opportunity.

Where the opportunity for hospitality exists— so does the opportunity to make a neighbor of a stranger.

In the monastery there are periods that call us to be a novice, a learner, to consider a new way of life, to begin a path. We don't come fully into a thing without effort. To say yes to the call of hospitality is to move toward it and to live it daily in the simple ways we encounter others. We need not go looking for chances to invoke hospitality upon the unsuspecting. Instead, we only need to consider the discovery of a neighbor in the stranger.

If we are going to reach the people who need the message of the gospel we will need to loosen our grasp on our churches. We hold too tightly to our idea of church, as well as to the buildings and programs. As individuals, we do the same with our lives. We clutch the familiar tightly and protect ourselves from anything or anyone that is unlike us. We guard ourselves from the threat of a well-intentioned neighbor.

We cannot journey down the gospel road this way. Instead, throw open the windows, swing wide the doors, crank up the music of our lives and our congregations. Amazing things will happen if we stop protecting ourselves and become available to others, radically available.

radical

hospitality

one

To Make a Beginning

hy are you interested in hospitality? Maybe you are happiest when sharing your table, or your space, with a guest. Maybe you yearn for connections to others. Maybe you are startled by the deep well of cynicism you've discovered in yourself and you want to stop keeping people at a distance. Maybe you, like many others, are looking for ways to heal from the horrors of past abuses and atrocities. Maybe you're curious about monasticism and the spirituality of monasticism.

Monasticism has much to teach us about welcoming and connecting with others. In exploring the deeper meaning of hospitality in these pages, I will be using the Benedictine path of hospitality as a model. Hospitality is at the center of what it means to be a monk.

The monk is something of an archetype for one who is at peace, one who has centered into where they live, what they do, and who they are becoming. If you've known monks, you know that the real thing and the image are nothing alike. The monk needed a rule because he is as likely as you and me to struggle, resist, and resent.

We are created to serve God by loving and serving one another. We do so through clenched teeth with hushed mutterings and curses. Monks too. To be a monk means that other people are sometimes crammed down your throat as they join you at table, at prayer, and as they want and need something from you, seemingly wanting to rip a chunk off of you. Sounding familiar yet?

You have your own reasons for being interested in the subject of welcoming others, and it may or may not have anything to do with spirituality. However, I think it's impossible to discuss true hospitality without delving into spirituality. Real hospitality isn't about what we do—it's about who we are.

Spirituality is essential to this discussion because spirituality is essential to what it means to be human. The human spirit is home to our deepest desires and darkest fears. It is also the place from which you yearn for a hand that will reach for yours. We both want and fear connecting with each other. Our resistance to others, resistance to change—these are housed in the mysterious realm of spirit. Our minds cannot conceive of solutions to our dilemma until our hearts are convinced to love. Because our ambivalence over connections with others is a problem of the heart and the spirit, the discussion will be largely spiritual.

When St. Benedict wrote of hospitality, he stressed the importance of welcoming the outsider, the poor, the pilgrim. Benedict understood that guests are crucial to the making of a monk. At the same time, we dare not view the guest as a tool in our spiritual development. Never, ever is the monk to understand hospitality as utilitarian; he should always see it as a welcoming of the Christ among us.

Benedict was a realist; he knew there would always be people at the monastery door. This was not a dreary reality for which he had to make allowances; it was a means of grace given to his monks, and he taught them how this complicated reality contributed to the making of a heart.

Guests are crucial to the making of any heart. Benedict instructed his monks to welcome the Divine in the stranger. He told them to look again, look deeper when you look into the eyes of stranger. If you want to be a person of great spirit, you can't do life alone. If spirituality matters to you, you can't do spirituality alone either. To really grow as a human being you need other people. This conviction permeates not only Benedict's Rule but all of Christianity, and in any place where community is intentional.

The monasteries of Benedict's time, fifteen centuries ago, were small. Usually they housed about a dozen monks, making the monastery something like a large family. They gathered as a Christian household to live and grow toward the Divine together. To guide them in this effort, Benedict crafted a simple, short document called *The Rule of St. Benedict*. It is no more than nine thousand words long and seventy-three short pages. An average person can read it in about an hour. The Rule has endured for the past fifteen hundred years and shapes most of Western monasticism. For this reason, St. Benedict is considered by most to be the father of Western monasticism.

Hospitality is at the center of what it means to be a monk, but Benedict didn't come up with the idea. The Rule is based on the teachings of Jesus. Jesus. Not a new improved guru for the new millennium, but the same old Jesus that the church has tried to follow for two thousand years.

A while back, on a chilly Minnesota day, a little boy was leaving a Christmas service with his father and paused at the manger outside the church. He looked at it, tilted his head for another angle, and then said to his father, "It's the same Jesus we had last year. Can't we get a new Jesus?" The father smiled and squatted next to his son. He was silent a couple of seconds and then said, "Son, we're Christians. We get the same Jesus every Christmas. That's how it works."

In monasticism you don't get a trendy new Jesus, you get the same old Jesus everyone gets. That's how it works. The monks who have become spiritual and social guides for so many are not practicing a new religion; they practice a very old one, the religion based on the life of Jesus. The notion of being trendy in any way would make most monks cringe. Benedict wrote the Rule within the context of his Christian faith, and so his teachings cannot be separated from the teachings of Jesus.

The word *rule* is something of a problem for us. We automatically resist rules. It is a symptom of contemporary life. Try thinking about it this way: A rule is nothing more than a set of ideas to help you determine the kind of person you will be and the course of your life. These ideas will be the reason you form certain habits (exercising, paying your bills on time, eating toast in the morning, meditating, and so on).

We all have some sort of rule we live by, consciously or otherwise. Your own rule consists of the little things you do that shape your life. The desire for balance or inner calm, the yearning for a life that feels right: these are the reasons we live by some kind of collected wisdom. Your rule of life is nothing more than what you have determined is most important to seeking and maintaining a meaningful existence. Your rule is a collection of what you think matters: I must be faithful to my friends, I must exercise, I must save money, I must take a couple of hours each week to be alone, I must make time to be with the people I love.

Your rule is what makes your life worthwhile. It is an expression of how you are spending your energy. It indicates what you value most. Your rule is the glue that holds your life together. It is the alarm that rings when your life is coming apart. By your rule, you make choices about how you will spend time and resources; you make choices about how you spend yourself.

In a monastery, where people come together as strangers from a wide variety of backgrounds, some sort of unifying system is necessary. That is the purpose of Benedict's Rule.

Through the years I have been part of and have observed various experiments and experiences of community. In the years before Facebook, I was (with Jane Frith, the list owner, and Will Westerfield, who was not only a facilitator but a tech wiz) a facilitator on an e-mail list titled Oblate Forum. We were an international group, ecumenical and diverse in all possible ways. We had a common focus, though—Benedictine spirituality based on *The Rule of St. Benedict*. It would seem that such a common focus would have created some semblance of harmony among us. It did not.

As forum leaders, we spent a great deal of time dealing with the egos, prejudices, agendas, and general nastiness from some of our forum members. There was no real consequence if someone invoked our displeasure; these were adults. We could only call people back to the organizing principle. We would use the Rule to remind people of our common goals; we would remind them that they agreed to certain rules when they joined the group. And then it would go well for a little while before another flare-up of ignorance and self-seeking behaviors occurred.

Generally, I was all for tossing the badly behaving members off the list. Jane was always more patient, more a peacemaker; Will was always more understanding and analytical. They would give people second and third chances. I could not escape my own impatience and intolerance in community with those hundreds of persons who were, in theory, like-minded. Community revealed to me the truth about myself.

The Rule in a monastery holds the place together. It is a central, organizing wisdom for monks who are trying to build a life together that points toward God. The Rule provides guidance, and it interprets gospel values in a way that is distinctive to Benedictines. In a family, we would probably consider the values shared by a couple a similar commonality upon which a life can be built.

The Rule of St. Benedict is not a set of legalistic rules or laws. We miss the essence of this ancient writing when we approach it in some literalistic sense. Rather, it is a collection of wisdom that has endured the hard blows of constant change in the last fifteen hundred years. There is no shortage of monastic rules, but only Benedict's Rule has thrived. It is uncomplicated wisdom that can build a life and expand a heart.

Many ways of life nurture the practice of hospitality. Monasticism isn't the only model. Many people who have never heard of Benedict practice a deep hospitality. I do not mean to claim that any of the strengths described here are unique to monasticism. Monasticism is a path, a choice that honors the presence of God in all our lives. Respect for human beings is not merely taught by the Benedictine tradition; it comes to life within the person who attempts to enter the tradition. In these pages, I hope to open a door to a hospitable way of life.

The Rule of St. Benedict begins with an invitation to listen. "Listen carefully, my child, to the instructions of the spiritual master, and attend to them with the ear of your heart. This is advice from a father who loves you; welcome it, and faithfully put it into practice."

This is the core of monastic life. *Listen.* At the beginning, you are invited to open your ears, open your heart, and listen for wisdom, listen for a Voice, listen for the *more* that is woven into all that is. This is the invitation and the call: listen.

Benedictine spirituality has a distinct ethos, which is learned through contact with the monks, through engaging with their way of life. Not everyone has a monastery down the road, however, so in these pages I would like to introduce you to St. Benedict Monastery, where Father Dan, a Roman Catholic monk and priest, lives. You'll meet some of the other brothers and priests. I hope you'll enter the pages and make the monastery your home for a little while.

The individuals in the community of monks are, like your own family or community, as distinct and different as individuals can be. They are gifted in many ways with strengths they bring to their community. Most have faults they also bring to their community. They are wonderfully human; they are tragically human.

St. Benedict Monastery is located in Oxford, Michigan, several miles up a gravel road that weaves toward the top of a hill at about twelve hundred feet above sea level. The setting was a glorious one long before religious orders constructed chapels and retreat houses on Drahner Road in Oxford. In addition to

St. Benedict Monastery, Drahner Road is home to St. Augustine's House, a Lutheran community also based on the Rule of St. Benedict. Native Americans spoke of the region as being sacred. Those who have learned to *listen* are often aware a sense of holiness in the setting.

One very endearing old monk, Father Noel, has been with God for several years now. His life was an example of Benedictine hospitality. Father Noel and Father Dan were taking a walk on the monastery grounds one day. It was the kind of day made for a walk with a friend. A group of eleven- and twelve-year-olds from an institution for troubled children were on a tour of the monastery. They had arrived by hay wagon, pulled by horses with a couple of young drivers, probably in their late teens.

Acres of rolling grass invite you to stretch out on a sultry summer day and enjoy the soft grass and warm earth. The monastery grounds are well groomed, but the place doesn't feel like an institution. It is home to the Benedictines, and a home is what it feels like— an easy place to be. Something about the place is welcoming.

The two monks were enjoying one of those long, warm days of late summer. Guests were not as common in those days, but when they showed up they were welcome. Occupied in conversation, Father Dan did not notice the hay wagon drivers until they came within a few yards.

"I was stopped in my tracks," he remembers. "Right there on the yard in front of us, the two wagon drivers were passing a joint back and forth, looking completely at home, as if this was the most natural thing to do at a monastery. In case you're wondering, it isn't."

Father Noel, born in Italy and a monk all of his adult life, had never seen marijuana. He was not a naïve or stupid man; such a thing simply was not part of his experience. Father Dan was a street smart kid raised in Detroit. Before he could demand an explanation, Father Noel spoke up.

"Young men," he exclaimed with wide-armed relish, "we are so glad that you are with us today to enjoy the grass."

It was an enthusiastic and heartfelt welcome from the hospitable soul of an old monk. The guys naturally thought he was one very cool old monk.

It would never have occurred to Father Noel to be suspicious of the young men. While many people would have considered them intruders, his welcome could not have been more sincere. He was delighted to see the children of God enjoying the expansive grounds. He was very happy to see someone enjoying the comforts of the cool, sweet grass of the monastery.

I met Father Noel when attending a friend's simple profession as a monk. A simple profession is the first set of vows a monk takes early in his monastic life. Following the solemn ceremony, a party that includes family and close friends is common. On this occasion, good friends of the monastic community had prepared a wonderful meal.

During dinner, I sat between the newly professed monk and Father Dan, who was seated between me and Father Noel. The chairs were squeezed together and if you swayed even slightly you bumped shoulders with the guest beside you. It was charming and jovial. Lively conversation was constant. Monks are wonderful conversationalists and storytellers.

Father Noel's Italian accent remained thick until the day he died, so, the hospitable thing to do, thought Father Dan, was to make sure that I understood precisely what Father Noel was saying to me. He was seated squarely between us and in the perfect spot for this particular role.

Throughout the meal, Dan translated Noel's conversation to me, usually in a whisper and with a bit of commentary. Meanwhile the older monk talked with a lively animation, smiling most of the time. Father Noel and I had never met before, and being Benedictine, he was eager to extend a welcome and get to know the guest in closest proximity. Hospitality is at the core of Benedictine spirituality, and Noel was Benedictine to the marrow.

After the dinner, Dan wandered off to greet other guests. He did not notice as Father Noel found me while I chatted with a small group of women. Father Dan did not notice Noel waiting for just the right moment when Dan could not interfere.

With a lovely wide smile, Father Noel took both my hands and said in quite nice English, "Now we can really talk, eh . . ." as he motioned with his head toward Dan, the obstacle during dinner. Father Noel did not need a middleman for his hospitality.

Regardless of being an introvert by nature, Noel's sense of hospitality had been fostered by a lifetime of making himself open to the stranger. To him, hospitality was not about social graces but about mutual reverence. Father Noel knew that spirituality is about relationships. Every man, woman, and child bears to us the presence of God.

Noel had the manners of man born in a certain European generation. He possessed the charm and the warmth. These are wonderful traits, but manners and civility are not at the heart of Benedictine hospitality, although we of course hope monks will not be rude or inconsiderate.

Hospitality does not focus on the goal of being hospitable. It is not about the one offering hospitality. Instead, it is singularly focused on the object of hospitality—the stranger, the guest, the delightful other. One of the inherent problems with programs to develop radical hospitality is the focus on hospitality as a goal. Hospitality requires that our focus is on the *other* rather than attainment of a concept.

Forget about turned down sheets, mints on the pillow, and towel warmers. Monastic hospitality creates sacred space where the guest is free to be alone, to enter silence, to pray and rest. No one is compelled to fill up the guest's spare time or set an agenda for him or her. Hospitality is openhanded. It's definitely not summer camp, but more like a refugee center for the traveler who needs shelter from thieves along the way.

If you are visiting a monastery and need someone to talk to, you will usually find an available ear, but they won't line up at your door to volunteer. The monks aren't there to keep anyone occupied or to be entertaining. Instead, Benedict tells us to offer an open heart, a stance of availability, and to look for God lurking in every single person who comes through the door. Monks do not consider themselves somehow polluted by contact with others. They aren't in a monastery to avoid people. This is a common misunderstanding of monastic life.

Monastic hospitality is devoted to the vision of unity among God's children. It is a necessary developmental vision for the monk because he will achieve no higher relationship with God, or others, than the one he achieves with himself. A monk's life presents us with a paradox. His life is a witness to us that, ultimately, we are all alone. We live and die alone. We wake up with only ourselves. We are never as fully understood and are never loved as well as we long to be.

On the other hand, the monk, to be a monk, needs people. He grows through encounters with others. He learns about himself as he is loved, annoyed, grieved, respected—all in community and with the guest. To think of the monk as only a solitary is a mistaken notion. There is a great truth to the monk as a solitary, as one who lives alone with God, but that aloneness is not lived apart. It is lived in community.

I was leading a retreat for a group of United Methodist women and their guests. It was an overnight event. As usual, I had scheduled a time of silence after dinner. Most retreatants find the silence of a retreat difficult the first time they enter it. But it wasn't true with this group. They sank into the silence as if it were a big, overstuffed chair where they were joyfully content to remain.

Later that evening, I spent some time in the retreat house library, where about fifteen women caught up with me. They were interested in silence and solitude as it was experienced in a monastery and how to take that into their everyday lives. The intensity of their seeking was unexpected, but not a surprise. We sense, on a soul level, that monasteries tell us something important about how to live in times like these.

Whether or not our ideas about monasteries are true, what the monastic life represents to us is the thing we seek after. Not just the silence or the solitude. I think it is less the cloister we crave and more the community. Maybe this is one of the reasons that churches and para-church organizations have been interested in radical hospitality. While the Rule of Benedict and monastic life are imperfect and human structures, it provides a starting place for the lessons in hospitality.

Monasticism was becoming popular, and you might even say monks were becoming trendy, prior to September 11, 2001. That event inspired much of the first edition of this book. We can no longer remember what the world was like before 9/11. For an entire generation, America lost her innocence that day. Within an hour of the collapse of the second tower of the World Trade Center, a woman on the streets of New York looked into a camera and said, "Nothing is ever going to be the same again."

Father Dan was in Rome watching those unforgettable events unfold. He heard the woman make the statement about nothing ever being the same and remembers thinking, "She's right, she's absolutely right, but I wish she were wrong."

We changed as a country and a community. Terror had come to our door. On September 10, 2001, it was considered spiritually enlightened to say,

"I'm a spiritual person but I'm not into organized religion." But when Americans needed an anchor, something to hold on to, they headed for the staying power of tradition. They filled churches, mosques, and synagogues in record numbers. Monasticism is undeniably part of organized religion. It has stood the test of time. America, traditionally, looks to what has endured, at a time when it seems the very foundations of the world are being rocked.

The events of September 11, 2001, are ten years behind us now. The chaos remains. In America we sense that something has struck at the foundation of what it means to be American. It is easy to blame this confusion and fear on the other, on the terrorists. But it is actually our response to terror that has shaped what and who we are becoming. We are created by our choices, and we create our world by those choices.

Benedict lived in the same kind of chaos. He wrote to a culture shaken to the core by the fall of the Roman Empire, fifteen hundred years ago. This makes Benedict particularly timely. People are now mining Benedictine spirituality to its depths for the profound wisdom that has made it relevant all these centuries.

The stranger next door, and at our door, is particularly frightening. I won't dodge the difficult reality of actual danger. People have been hurt by strangers. You need only to turn on the evening news to be aware that we are growing into a fearful people, suspicious of strangers and outsiders. Hospitality is risky, and it is scary.

I met a woman in Dayton, Ohio, who talked about the risks she takes in hospitality. She invites the homeless into her home. She is a widowed woman, around sixty, who has a big house in a quiet neighborhood.

"My family and friends worry," she admitted. "They think I'm taking too many risks. I tell them it's what I have to do. You know, I realize there's a risk. I live with the risk. I'm not foolish about having people into my house. They're always someone who knows someone who knows someone. Still, it's risky."

She says it is worth the risk and she has no regrets. Others consider what she does much too radical. She is compelled, though. She would even go so far as to say she is called.

Unless we find a way to open ourselves to others, we will grow even more isolated and frightened. If we do not find and practice ways of hospitality we will grow increasingly hostile. Hospitality is the answer to hostility. Jesus said to love your neighbor; hospitality is how.

The people we encounter daily, at the gas station and grocery store and flower shop, aren't incidental to our lives. Benedict teaches us that if we close ourselves to the stranger, we close ourselves to the Sacred. If we lock our doors and bolt our gates, we are forbidding God to come to us. And never before have we needed so badly to know that God comes to us.

Most of us have heard some version of the good Samaritan story from the Gospels of the New Testament. Jesus told a story. A traveler is accosted, robbed, beaten, and left to die. As he suffers on the side of the road, the dying man is ignored by the "right" kind of people, acceptable people with solid values and important priorities.

The people who ignore the dying man are like us. They have things to do. They are trying very hard to get it all done. They aren't vicious people, but they do consider caution a virtue.

It was the "wrong" kind of person, in the culture of the New Testament—a Samaritan—who stopped to help. The Samaritan went the extra mile and put himself on the line. He gave his time, energy, and resources. To the religious community, the good Samaritan was unclean, a stranger, and utterly unacceptable—and yet a model in hospitality.

The story is about us, and it is about strangers. We are called to be the kind stranger, to be kind to strangers, and to hold our breaths in wonder at the healing power of the stranger among us. The story is also a reminder that every one of us is going to be the one beaten up and waiting for healing at the side of the road. You don't have to live long before you realize that no one escapes pain.

We moderns have been ambushed by technology along the way, and we've been beaten up by the media. We, who are consumers, have discovered that in our constant consuming we are leaving little for anyone else, and we're losing our souls. We find ourselves scattered on the winds of change to places we never wanted to go. Our lives seem to be spinning out of control. It is no wonder we lock our doors and switch on the security system.

Fear is the mainstay of news, commerce, religion, media. Fear shapes our choices. Fear keeps us from living our lives freely. Terrorism could have elicited a different response if we were not a people of such deep fear. Could we have used the experience to ask ourselves how we can better live with our Muslim neighbors? How we have failed to be a global neighbor?

We have also lost our souls in the marketplace, in the bickering, the negotiating. Must we position ourselves as productive winners at all times? Go with me to a corner of the sprawling market in Mexico City where an old Indian man named Potalamo is selling onions. Twenty strings of onions lay in front of him. A guy from Denver walks up and asks, "How much for a string of onions?"

"Ten cents," replies Potalamo.

"How much for two strings?"

Potalamo fixes his eyes on him and says, "Twenty cents."

"What about three?"

"Thirty cents."

"Not much of a reduction for quantity. Would you take twenty-five cents for three?"

"No."

"Well, how much for all of it, the whole twenty strings?"

"I will not sell you the whole twenty strings."

"Why not?" asks the American. "Aren't you here to sell onions?"

"No," replies Potalamo, "I am here to live my life. I love this market. I love the crowds. I love the sunlight and smells. I love the children. I love to have my friends come by and talk about their babies and their crops. That is my life and for that reason I sit here with my twenty strings of onions. If I sell all my onions to one customer, then my day is over and I have lost my life that I love—and that I will not do."

Living life in a way that places a higher value on relationships and community than it does on commerce and productivity—this is counter to how most of us have been taught. We live our lives selling onions. There is no room for hospitality in a life like that. We greet the morning sun each day with our to-do lists, while the monk greets the sun with prayer and silence.

We hide out, isolate ourselves, and deny our natural need for others. We erroneously think we need safety the most. What we need most is acceptance. You probably can't understand me, and I might not understand you, but we can accept each other. We need to connect and feel the deep acceptance of another human being, and that will make the world feel safer. Locks and firewalls can never do for our tired souls what friendship and companionship do.

Acceptance. Now there's a word loaded with meaning. We tend to confuse it with tolerance or even approval. But acceptance is about receiving, rather than judging. The father who will not visit his son because his son is living unmarried with a woman, or even with another man, might say he doesn't want to condone his son's choices. We feel for him, but we know it's a cover-up because we, too, have rationalized our avoidance of things and situations we would rather not have to face. Then we can hide the disappointment, cover the anger, and justify the rejection. We struggle in our best efforts to hold back judgment and just accept. Acceptance is not about condoning; it is about embracing.

When we accept, we take an open stance to the other person. It is more than mere pious tolerance. We stand in the same space and we appreciate who they are, right now at this moment, and affirm the Sacred in them. Monks do this better than most.

I recall an acceptance from a priest a long time ago. He wasn't a monk, but the parish priest. I was six years old and days away from my First Communion. At rehearsal, the little group of us practiced processing in, found our places to stand, and practiced how to take the host and return to our seats without too much disruption.

My oldest brother Harry was one of the altar boys assigned to the event. After practice, the other kids had gone home. I needed to wait for Harry because we would walk home together. He told me to stay put in the front row of the sanctuary and he'd be back in a few minutes. Sit still, stay put—not an easy thing for a six-year-old girl to do. I watched him disappear through the sacristy door, wondering if he'd ever emerge from that place of wonders of mystery.

I had not been seated long when Father Lawrence, the parish priest, found me. I explained that I was waiting for Harry so we could walk home together.

"Oh. Well, he's going to be a while. He's watering my plants." (That was code for having a cigarette with the other altar boys—things were different fifty years ago.) Father Lawrence offered his hand, "Would you like to see the sacristy?"

How did he know, I wondered, that I wanted to see behind that closed door, that the mystery beckoned?

It was like the gates of heaven swinging open. My face must have told him the answer. He pulled me to my feet, held my hand tight, and together we headed toward the altar before I could get words out. That crazy priest even let me hold a chalice. A little girl. A girl, of all things.

Monks are a lot like old Father Lawrence. They strive to accept others totally—no, not perfectly, and not all the time—but they keep trying to take us into the hidden places and the holy mysteries we dream of knowing, but feel unprepared or unworthy to enter. It isn't that the monk has some special right to go into that place with us; it is just that a lifetime of facing himself makes a monk brave.

Monks break all our conventional rules in the way they accept and receive others. It is their tradition. One of my favorite examples of this is how St. Benedict told his followers that if you have to discipline someone make sure you send a couple of wise monks to comfort him and be on his side (you do this on the sly) and "support the wavering brother." "Remember," Benedict tells his monks, "you have undertaken care of the sick, not tyranny over the healthy." Benedict can seem tough and unrelenting, but he is unrelenting in love, acceptance, and reconciliation.

Hospitality tops the list of what is valued in a monastery because people are valued, and an equal dignity for all is assumed. Monks view people positively. Every human is sacred; every life is holy ground.

Many of the people who rattle the gates of St. Benedict Monastery arrive there in search of shelter. It was certainly true of my early experience with the monastery. It was a difficult time. My teenaged daughter had been in a debilitating near-fatal accident from which she came away with a closed head injury that would change her life forever. I was the target of vicious gossip, half-truths, and general meanness. I went to the monastery to visit a friend who had joined. I stayed because they took me in as well.

Outside those walls I watched church people attacking each other, attempting to destroy innocent people. The church that had once been family seemed to turn on me, on others. Nothing felt right. The world did not feel safe. Every trace of God was emptied from the universe. Each day I forced myself out of the bed. *Breathe in and out*, I would tell myself. *Keep moving.*

With the monks I was suddenly accepted—accepted during a time when I felt rejected, violated, misunderstood, and betrayed. I remained because these monks loved me without question. I didn't have to prove anything. I didn't have to be smart or witty, deep or cultured, beautiful or young. I just had to let them love me.

By accepting someone, we do what seems to be a small, ordinary thing. A single act would seem to be small, but little acts of giving, one upon another, pile up to create a huge force capable of repelling darkness and transforming the world. A friendly conversation with a stranger at a bus stop can be the embodiment of hospitality. When we accept a human being, we are fostering the kind of hospitality that will change everything. When we build a life of acceptance, we build a new kind of kingdom among us.

The monastic life has an essence that is worth observing, worth applying to your own complicated life. Yes, monastic lives are different, but not that different. Monks still have mouths to feed, windows to wash, groceries to buy, cars to repair, and complications to sort out. There are more similarities than differences.

The monk is not some otherworldly character; he's just a guy in a black robe who is trying very hard to be found by God.

A problem with using the monastic model as a guide for life is that it comes with language no one uses anymore. *Hospitality. Stability. Chastity. Poverty. Obedience.* Monks hold meetings they call diets, and they do not mean cutting calories. They have leaders who are called Primates and who don't live in the local zoo. What is a Prior? What does *the work of God* mean? How many ways can you use the word *cloister*?

I will try to be careful in using language that might be confusing. If you're familiar with things Benedictine this might seem unnecessary, but I ask you to remember the marvelous idea of hospitality as I attempt to make this book an open place for all of God's children.

Some might think of monasticism as too "traditional" to be of any meaning today. Especially as the sins of the Catholic Church continue to make news. In a world where the word *tradition* is nearly obscene, monasticism shows us how humanizing and freeing tradition can be. Through tradition we receive the wisdom of those who have gone on before us. Tradition underscores that which we must not forget. Tradition is valuable, not because it is old and established but because it has endured and brought about much that is good.

Yet, there is always the possibility of the new and untried, of seeing the old in a new light. In fact, Benedict makes clear in the Rule that young people have something important to offer, and it is vital that we listen to the young with all their fresh ideas. The Benedictine way of life and hospitality is full of openness and risk.

Benedict's conviction was that all of us are headed together toward God. We are headed toward union with God. It is impossible to say what this means exactly, but we live our little lives with big purpose and a sense that there is more. We do this by faith. It goes against the seeming ordinariness of everything. We take a radical position when we insist that it all *does* matter. Life is holy ground.

Now be careful about this. Holy ground is dangerous. It is the region of thundering mountains and burning bushes; it is the domain of men and women bellowing prophecy with fire in their wings and the winds of change in their voices.

A friend from Alaska has said that lots of people visit the state in pursuit of great beauty and breathless awe. Expecting to be tackled by wonder and to experience some earth-shattering majesty, these people encounter long stretches of treacherous roads and miles of what looks like frozen desert. It teems with hidden dangers—like bears. After one couple was mauled, they told a reporter that they would never return to "this godforsaken" place. Holy places put you at risk more so than any other place. You feel both at risk and awed in a holy place.

In 1982, author Annie Dillard witnessed a total eclipse of the sun and described the experience:

> The second before the sun went out, we saw a wall of dark shadow come speeding at us. We no sooner saw it than it was upon us, like thunder. It roared up the valley. . . . Seeing it, and knowing it was coming straight for you, was like feeling a slug of anesthetic shoot up your arm. . . . We saw the wall of shadow coming, and screamed before it hit us.
>
> Less than two minutes later, when the sun emerged . . . We blinked into the light. . . . We

never looked back. It was a general vamoose . . .
enough is enough. . . . *

Life is a lot like that hilltop. We gather together
to have the hell scared out of us, literally. We catch a
glimpse of each other, we sense the smell of God, and
although we rush away from the holiest of moments,
we are utterly changed. Life slams us into God, and
if we have any sense knocked into us, we realize that
behind all the ordinary stuff there is something more
dazzling and real than we can understand. Life is holy
ground. Holy ground is risky.

Benedict understands holy ground. Life is holy
ground and so are the monastery, the monk, and
the guest. The monastery is not personal property; it
belongs to God. Your life is not personal property;
you belong to God. Benedict called the monastery
God's house. The monks own nothing, they are simply
stewards of whatever God gives them. In this vision,
even the monks are guests, and so Benedict insists that
the monks "serve one another in love." "Never give

---

* *The Annie Dillard Reader* (New York: Harper Perennial,
1995), 15–16.

a hollow greeting of peace," he writes, "or turn away when someone needs your love."

At the monastery everyone is a guest, not just the visitor at the door, but the monks themselves. God is the host, but God also becomes the guest we receive in others. In the monastic image of the world, we are all guests, we are all travelers, we are all a little lost, and we are all looking for a place to rest a while.

A journey is one of the most common metaphors for life. We understand the image contains some strong truth. Life is very much like a journey. In our quiet moments, when we let down our guard, we become aware that we are looking for something, going somewhere, even though most of the time we cannot say where.

Even if you are born, grow up, and die in the same house in which your parents and grandparents spent their lives, life is still a journey. Saint Benedict wrote from his conviction that life truly is a journey and we are all co-travelers who need one another if we are to get home.

Every moment is more brightly precious than we can possibly understand. Our lives are worth more than the best deal that might tempt you to sell your soul. We did not bargain for most of what we get in this life, but life itself is worth holding on to and worth valuing. It is a great loss if we greet every day with clenched hands stuffed with our own devices. We will never know what is out there waiting for us if we don't extend an empty hand to the world and wait for the wonder to happen. Benedictine hospitality provides us with a way to offer empty hands to the world. It provides us with a way home.

Sometimes we get so lost that we need a map. Without a point of reference we keep stumbling in circles with little awareness of where we've been or how to reach where we are going. Monastic life provides one such point of reference. It provides us a way to find our way back to Love, when that possibility seems about as remote as the North Pole.

A doctor told me that when patients are desperately ill, suffering great pain, or dying, they often call out for their mother. It is the call of the heart to go home again, to return to its source, to wrap its final breath in the memory of being loved. Love is the best memory of our wayward hearts. We are looking for what our heart already knows. The way back, whispers Benedict, is this way. Come follow and I will show you the way of hospitality.

two

The Taming of Hospitality

atherine had never felt accepted. You know the kind of kid; you went to school with a few of them. It was as if she had been selected the very first day of kindergarten to be always on the outside. Maybe she was wearing mismatched mittens one day, or she still had peanut butter on her breath from breakfast. Maybe she wore the same shoes her sister wore last year. Father Dan never knew the reason for her being the social outcast she was. By the time he met her on retreat, she was firmly in place as the target for the teenaged sport of ridicule.

Without knowing the details, you can be sure that Catherine spent a lot of very tough nights growing up. She must have wondered if her life meant anything and wondered if anyone would ever listen to her. She probably did not dare hope that she would ever be loved. It is hard to imagine, if you've never been the one on the outside, what it can do to you. Just getting out of bed each morning becomes an act of courage.

On one of the worst nights of her life, Catherine called Mary Cummings, Father Dan's partner in retreat ministry. She called Mary because once, when Catherine had dropped books and whatever else she was carrying, Mary stopped and helped. Mary extended the simplest of courtesies to this girl that had known only contempt. By taking a moment to look into her eyes, say a few words, and help in an awkward situation, Mary demonstrated to Catherine that she could be counted on to care. On the night when Catherine honestly did not know if she wanted to see another sunrise, she called Mary.

When we speak of hospitality we are always addressing issues of inclusion and exclusion. Each of us makes choices about who will and who will not be included in our lives. To make such choices is inevitable; we do not have time to be everyone's best friend. The reasons we include and exclude are very personal. You and I probably can't even say why we become close to some people and have no interest in getting to know, or include, others. We only know that we prefer some, and others are harder to like.

Issues of inclusion and exclusion, while personal, are not just personal. Our entire culture excludes many people. If you are in a wheelchair, for example, you are excluded because there are places you can't go. If you are very young, if you are very old, you are excluded. In high school you can be excluded if you don't wear the right shoes or listen to the right music. Women are excluded, as are people of color and those who practice a religion different from our own.

In our idealism about American life the poor are always excluded; they are our embarrassing little American secret. The American dream has failed the one in six children living in poverty. These children will, most likely, grow up to a lifetime of exclusion. Somewhere, sometime, you were excluded. Remember what that was like. Some people live with the experience constantly.

There was a common saying in Germany just before the Nazi reign: "The human body contains a sufficient amount of fat to make seven cakes of soap, enough iron to make a medium-sized nail, a sufficient amount of phosphorus for two thousand matchheads, enough sulfur to rid one person of fleas."

The Nazi view of humanity reduced us to nothing more than the usefulness of our physical components, and when that was used up it was fine to cast aside the human being.

But you and I are much more than what we appear to be. We are more than what we do. We are more than a social or economic class. In the movie *Elephant Man*, actor John Merrick is chased through a train station and cornered in a bathroom by a mob that sees only his deformity, his difference from them. He cries out, "I am not an animal. . . . I am a human being. . . ."

This is the sound of every single human heart. It is the cry we make against all that would make us less human, the cry of the darkest night of our lives, the cry of the abandoned and the misunderstood and the excluded. "I am not an animal. I am like you. I am human."

I am not a street person.
I am not a token of my race or creed.
I am not a statistic.
I am not a divorcée.

I am not an AIDS patient.

I am not a sex object.

I am not a laborer.

I am not an "at risk" kid.

I have a mind. I have a heart. I have a soul. I dream.

I feel. I care. I am a human being.

Hospitality has an inescapable moral dimension to it. It is not a mere social grace; it is a spiritual and ethical issue. It is an issue involving what it means to be human. All of our talk about hospitable openness doesn't mean anything as long as some people continue to be tossed aside.

In a 1982 report, one ethicist put it this way: "The opposite of cruelty is not simply freedom from the cruel relationship, it is hospitality." Hospitality puts an end to injustice. But calling hospitality a moral issue does not tell us the whole truth about hospitality either. A moral issue can become bogged down in legalisms, and hospitality is no legalistic ethical issue. It is instead a spiritual practice, a way of becoming more human, a way of understanding yourself. Hospitality is both the answer to modern alienation and injustice *and* a path to a deeper spirituality.

As a culture, we are frightened people living behind locked doors, fashioning our homes as reclusive retreats from what we believe is a hostile world that sits at our door. The world at our gate is a fearsome thing. We lock the doors, click on the security system, put on headphones, and enter a place where we hope to be left to ourselves but always keep an ear listening for the sound of disturbance. It's no surprise that we are lonelier than ever before.

If thousands of people can be laughing with a friend, walking to work, or getting ready for an appointment at their desk when they are annihilated, how can we feel safe anywhere, anytime? We can't make light of this reality, but neither do we need to live in fear.

How do we keep from fearing the stranger? How do you and I look into the eyes of the stranger and conjure up acceptance for him? In the days following the September 11 attacks on New York and Washington, you may recall a lot of people talking about their nervousness and growing suspicion with the dark-skinned stranger, the one who talks a bit Middle Eastern, the one who has been their neighbor. In the last ten years we have not become less fearful. The passage of time has dulled our memories but sharpened our fears.

A couple months after the attack, I visited Ground Zero with my oldest daughter. We met a man from Dublin who had worked very near the Twin Towers for twelve years. He told us that he hated the people "who did this terrible thing," and he wept. Then, in the next breath he gazed up to heaven and said, "You see, we are all the children of God, made in his very own image, and that makes it unbearable. The hating has to stop. 'Tis sadder than words can say."

'Tis. And in the days and years that have followed many sad things happened.

You may remember that in some instances the person with feared ethnic characteristics was removed from planes by passenger request, regardless of their innocence. People who were part of a community, who had been considered neighbors, suddenly became suspect, even if your kids went to school together and you bowled together on Tuesday night.

Two of the monks at St. Benedict Monastery are rather dark-skinned and would appear Middle Eastern to those who do not know their actual ancestry. Father Damien is Albanian; Brother Antony is from Puerto Rico. Often, they have been teased by their brother monks about looking like terrorists in their driver's license pictures. It had been good-natured teasing, but is no longer funny.

Imagine the difficulty these men have getting on a plane, or the discomfort they cause others. Two of the biggest hearts on the planet, two of the greatest spirits, and if either of them sits beside you on an airplane your heart will probably fall to your stomach and your pulse will race. You will want them removed; at the very least you will want them double-checked. You could not find two safer human beings if you scoured the universe, yet they are suddenly suspect because of skin color and ethnic features.

The events of terrorism have created a new dark filter through which we view the world. After ten years, this is still true. We comfort ourselves by thinking, "But it isn't an unreasonable fear. Some awful things have happened and they have been done by men who look a certain way." Contrary to the comforting lies we tell each other, this kind of fear *is* unreasonable.

Every person of Middle Eastern descent is not responsible for the big, awful thing that happened. Timothy McVeigh did not cause people to fear every white male, not unless you already thought white guys were dangerous.

The horror of September 11, 2001, did not create bigotry against Muslims; it incited existing bigotry. It fed a silently held bigotry already alive in a dark corner of our hearts. It uncapped a quietly seething suspicion that has continued to feed off fear and ignorance. It is easier to fear a whole group of people instead of giving one person a chance. It becomes easy to hate and to turn away from people we have vilified.

To live courageously means giving up the fear and giving every single person a chance. "The home of the brave" is a wonderful ideal, but it is no easy thing to become. Brave people take a risk with the stranger. Brave people offer up their hearts, again, after they've pieced together the fragments of a broken heart. Brave people don't let themselves off the hook when something has gone wrong inside of them.

Fear is a thief. It will steal our peace of mind, and that's a lot to lose. But it also hijacks relationships, keeping us sealed up in our plastic world with a fragile sense of security. Being a people who fear the stranger, we have drained the life juices out of hospitality. The hospitality we explore here is not the same kind you will learn about from Martha Stewart. Benedictine hospitality is not about sipping tea and making bland talk with people who live next door or work with you. Hospitality is a lively, courageous, and convivial way of living that challenges our compulsion either to turn away or to turn inward and disconnect ourselves from others.

Hospitality is not optional to a well-balanced and healthy life. It meets the most basic need of the human being to be known and to know others. It addresses the core loneliness that we avoid with the bustle and haste of our hectic lives. There is a big loneliness at the center of every person. It is universal. There's a reason for the loneliness. It is meant to lead you somewhere. Even if you are unconscious of it, the big lonely is driving you homeward.

Hospitality has two meanings for most people today. It either refers to hotels and cruise ships, or it is connected to entertaining friends and family in the warmth of candlelight with gleaming silver and ivory lace. One model makes it an industry, thereby assigning some productive use to it and making it profitable. The other model relegates it to the domain of entertainment and housekeeping, generally considered women's work. Thus it has become safe and cozy, even productive, rather than revolutionary, risky, and world rattling.

Benedictine hospitality does not allow us to turn people into a profit-making venture, nor are goodness and graciousness deemed suitable only for the cozy small world of our private homes and feminine natures. Benedict finds God in people. You can't ignore people when God is looking out their eyes at you. In the tiresome, the invalid, the rebellious, we are faced with God. It is our own failures to love that we have to deal with when we talk of hospitality. Hospitality cuts through the sham of our excuses.

Benedict is a realist about loving. He knows love comes only through effort and practice. It is costly. It is fatiguing. It is not some warm, fuzzy feeling Benedict wants us to conjure up; he wants the strength of respect and reverence to beat in the hearts of his monks.

When we are filled with prejudice, suspicion, anxiety, or jealousy, we have no room for welcoming, for listening or receiving. The monastic life allows the monk to empty himself of the darker impulse—not that he is ever completely rid of it, but he actively resists in the sharing of the table and the embracing of strangers.

Hospitality did not begin with Howard Johnson's and *Good Housekeeping*. Hospitality, as it has been practiced from ancient days, protected people from the dangers of traveling alone. In Saint Benedict's day there were no safe and cheap shelters for travelers. Along the way people could be brutalized, robbed, wounded, lost.

Monasteries saved lives when they opened their doors to strangers. It was not about comfort and entertainment—it was about saving lives. A little dramatic? Well, it seems that way today when we have a Marriott on every corner, shelters for the homeless and the battered, and hostels around the world.

This spirit of saving lives is still at the root of monastic hospitality. To receive others is to expose myself to all sorts of frightful dangers of attachment and rejection. Hospitality acknowledges the vulnerability of being human, both my humanity and that of the stranger. Travelers, too (Benedict called them pilgrims), are prone to all sorts of dangers. On life's journey each of us is a pilgrim. We aren't sure where we came from and where we are going. We are vulnerable and we need each other.

Some of the most moving stories of hospitality have come out of the Holocaust. One Dutch woman, who now lives in a small Michigan town, told of growing up in a household that sheltered a Jewish family. All such stories are inspiring and remarkable, but hers was especially so because her parents kept the secret so well that their four children did not know a Jewish family was sheltered in their home. The parents risked everything to protect strangers, literal strangers, whose presence threatened them and their children.

This kind of sacrificial hospitality is almost more than we can imagine. We will probably never be called on to give ourselves for the sake of a stranger—but can we give some small part of ourselves to a stranger? We probably will never have to build a secret room in our homes to save the lives of people we don't know—but can we carve out a small place in our hearts for others? This is the true meaning of hospitality.

Monasteries are increasingly making room for strangers, by planning their lives to allow room for guests. This hospitality is included in the Benedictine rule, but it is also the current reality of monasteries. People are knocking on the door. People of all faiths or no faith at all are drawn to something about monasticism. The challenge for Benedictines is to preserve their monastic distinction, their way of life, while continuing to welcome the stranger. It is similar to the challenge you face as you attempt to keep time for yourself and your closest relationships while developing an open attitude.

The walking dead stand at the gates of the monastery. If life doesn't kill your wonder, it will at least wound your spirit. The monastic way is sometimes called the path of life, and life is what we seek. People go to the monastery in search of life. Today, Benedictines are not physically saving lives by their tradition, but they do continue to save lives in other ways. The spirit of monastic hospitality gives us something healing and rejuvenating. So, while hospitality has changed in practice since Benedict's day, the lifesaving spirit of it has remained.

Those of us who don't live in monasteries have lost the practice of hospitality itself, as well as an open spirit that welcomes others. Not only our homes, but also we, like the monastery, need to become a place of solace and safety. Benedictine spirituality insists that if you want to be whole, you have to let the other in.

The missing virtue of our era has been turned into a social grace that neither disturbs nor transforms. That is not what Benedict meant when he shaped a way of life that would value at its deepest core, then and now, a life of hospitality.

Today, we take to ourselves only those we have met at work or in our neighborhood. We eat with our family. We lunch with our friends. If we ever include a stranger, it had better be a stranger that someone can vouch for. The outcast, the foreigner, the unacceptable person, these we avoid with a tight fear that chokes the life out of what it means to be hospitable.

You protest. There is very real danger in the stranger. Open the house and open a threat to my sleeping children? Open the door and violence enters. What about all the kooks with a knife? You read the countless horror stories with tragic endings. You aren't making all this stuff up; it is real and only a fool would ignore the dangers. In this culture, is it possible to recover the gentle art of hospitality? Is there a way to enliven it, to recreate it so that personal safety is not at risk, but still the stranger is welcomed and honored? A lofty goal? Probably, but worth the effort.

It is worthwhile for no other reason than this: When I consider the stranger, I am faced with my worst fears. I can't deny that I am afraid and that I don't even always like people.

Many years ago I considered a vocational change that would put me, a fierce introvert, into constant contact with others. I don't do small talk and I rarely speak to strangers. I harbor a deep well of cynicism that keeps most people from getting too close. In the vocation I was considering, people would be unavoidable.

The vocational counselor listened to my concerns, and then said with unhidden bewilderment, "I know you're sincere in pursuing this path, but I really don't understand what makes you think you'd be good at this—you don't even like people all that much."

It was said with kindness and a twinkle in the counselor's eye. Hyperbole sometimes makes the point best. For me, learning to like people will be the work of a lifetime. I have my reasons for not trusting. If you could get into my heart for ten minutes you'd understand. The counselor was right, though. Despite my many logical and emotional reasons for cynicism, it would not have been a good choice for me.

On a daily basis, in small ways, I confront all of the mess that has made me back away from people. By making even a small effort, hospitality allows me to do the difficult thing and that's always good for the soul.

Once you get over linking hospitality to the travel industry and dinner parties you still have to deal with that awkward reality of strangers. Hospitality involves accepting responsibility to care for the strangers, the ones at our gate, but also those a world away.

The biggest obstacle to hospitality is not the state of the world. It is the state of our minds and hearts. It is the comfort we crave so badly that we will do almost anything for it.

Benedictine hospitality prevents us from living either desperately or indifferently. Hospitality requires not grand gestures, but open hearts. When I let a stranger into my heart, I let a new possibility approach me. When I reach past my own ideas, I begin to stretch myself open to the world, and this opening of my heart could change everything. That's pretty frightening stuff. You can't ever be the same if you start doing that kind of thing.

My response will be different from yours and different from a monk's. Relating to others always involves the patterns you have learned in other relationships. Hospitality comes easily for those who have known mostly acceptance and love. For other people, it will come harder.

A friend told me a story from his recent illness:

> When I was very ill, it was necessary to receive frequent intravenous treatments, injections, blood tests, and many intrusive medical

treatments. At first I had the courage for it, but day after day I lost courage, until the day a small Korean woman, the head nurse, walked into my hospital room after several failed attempts to find a vein. I glared at her, pushed her hand away, and said, "I can't take this anymore."

She nodded and held my hand, and we sat in the quiet for a minute or so. Then, she said, "I just finished injecting medication into a permanent port in the belly of a twelve-year-old boy who will probably die before the year is over. I could not take what I do if it weren't for the fact that sometimes what I do saves a life." I extended my arm and gave her my vein.

No, it is not easy to give your vein. Even when you know it is for your own good, you also know there's going to be pain involved. The things we'll do to avoid pain. There is a lot of pain that goes with relationships and we never quite recover from some of it, but the pain you're carrying around is not needless or pointless. It can be used to save a life. No, you would not have volunteered for it. But it could save a life, and that's worth it.

Maybe you are one of the fortunate people who find hospitality easy. If so, you can probably look back to definite times you felt connected to others and well loved. If you have experienced abiding and strong relationships, hospitality comes more easily. I once asked a student to write about a friendship she remembered:

I remember my first loss of a friend, but it isn't the loss that has stayed with me, it is the friendship. My best friend Terry and I were seven. She lived next door, but next door was down the street a little ways. You walked through a maze of brush, a maze carved out by my brother and his pals who liked to play fort in that brush. The brush was a jungle to the boys, but to us it was the enchanted forest where our friendship grew. Terry and I shared everything, our toys and books, our rooms and our families. We shared our dreams, too.

We promised that when we grew up, we would have houses next door to one another in the mountains we had seen in pictures. She would have a big barn for her horses; I would have a big library for my books. It was the summer of our seventh year and I was sure that, no matter what, we would be friends. I didn't see circumstances beyond our control approaching.

Her father was in the Coast Guard and he was being moved. No matter how much I wanted it, she could not take me with her and I could not keep her with me. Years passed and I have never seen Terry again. And while she hasn't told me a joke in fifteen years, the laughter remains. We haven't held hands to walk past the bully, but the strength lives on. We haven't raced and danced in our enchanted forest but life has seemed enchanted ever since. We never built those houses in the mountains, but I think of her when I see a mountain. When you have a friend, you have the best this life has to give.

A friendship like that will make you the kind of person who is able to be hospitable. Hospitality is born in us when we are well loved by God and by others. Hospitality is the overflowing of a heart that has to share what it has received. It takes a whole person to open up, it takes a secure person to be available, it takes a strong person to give yourself away.

It is possible to serve meals in a nursing home, to cook in a homeless shelter, or to read stories to children at an inner-city library and never let others into your heart. It is possible to do the good thing and end up feeling satisfied with yourself and even just a bit superior. It is possible to do the good thing and not be changed for the better by it. Hospitality includes cooking the meal and reading to the kid, but it demands that you let the people you are serving into your heart. Only in opening yourself wide to another are you transformed by the power of love.

If you are already thinking of ways to be more hospitable, just slow down. Don't worry just yet about opening up your door; focus on opening your heart. Do not worry about the time involved or how you can make it happen. Instead, look inside and see if you can find an empty space where you can let someone in.

Merely being nice to people does not fulfill the deep requirements of Benedictine hospitality. We must let the person stir us; we must connect. Benedictine hospitality will extract a cost from us, and it will tumble us into the magical realm of personal transformation.

Opening yourselves to the stranger is not equivalent to leaving your door unlocked and bringing strangers into your home. Hospitality does not mean you ignore obvious threats to personal safety. Hospitality means bringing strangers into your heart, which may or may not result in inviting strangers to the table. Do not harden your heart against suffering. Widen your boundaries to include those who are not like you. When monks open up their monastery, they are making a place for someone who is not one of them. You and I, we are the strangers at the door of the monastery.

We take our rumbling fears and hopes, our silent regrets, our dumb ideas, and our half-formed selves with us to the monastery. We are complicated strangers, not always easy to love strangers. One friend of the monastery remembers going there late one afternoon. It was one of those days. You know the kind. The world is spinning too fast and your soul is too slow. One of those days when someone has ripped off the last chunk of you and there's nothing left.

She was new to the monastery. She didn't know the schedule—when the monks prayed, when they ate meals. She would have been more considerate of the pattern of their life together, but she didn't know. Because of this, she showed up that stormy, spring afternoon just as the monks were finishing Vespers and readying for dinner.

She didn't call first. She just aimed her car toward the monastery, the only place in the world that seemed safe.

The retreat house was jammed with teenagers on retreat. Father Dan and the staff were enormously occupied with the teens. When she arrived, she parked her car and started walking, nearly blind with tears. She walked down to the pond and walked back. She stood at the fence and watched the cows.

"I'm not sure what I was doing there or what I expected," she remembers. "I knew it was a safe place. I just felt that if I got there, somehow I would be better for it. I felt that I'd get help in handling the tangle of feelings and painful emotions.

"I got out of my car and walked around a little. There are several buildings on the monastery grounds. The monastery is across the driveway from the retreat house. I tried not to give in to the tears that burned my eyes, but I wasn't succeeding. I was friends with one of the monks and maybe I thought he'd materialize out of thin air, but he was off praying and dining with his brother monks."

She didn't see the storm gathering over her head. She remained at the fence, watching the cows, silent, waiting for something she could not name.

She continues, "A hand descended on my shoulder and I turned to look into the smiling, concerned face of Father Dan. He didn't know me well. We'd met only a time or two after mass. His eyes quickly took in my tearstained face, and he asked without prelude if I would like him to fetch my friend or did I want to be alone? The man had fifty teenagers in the retreat house doing God only knows what, as he stood at the edge of the cow pasture with me. I replied that I wasn't sure. Not a particularly helpful response to his question. He said, 'Please, come inside then,' and motioned toward the retreat house. On the way inside I noticed large threatening clouds gathering in the evening sky. Not only was he concerned about what I was feeling, he wanted to get me out of the elements, too. Once inside, he put a cup of hot chocolate in my hand and said, 'The monks are having dinner. Can I get you something to eat? We have pizza here at the retreat house. His voice was edged with anxiety. He offered me everything short of a pot roast. He wanted to ease the pain.

"He must have recognized that he was overwhelming me a bit because he fell silent, sat with me, and allowed me to collect myself. Then I told him

I would like to talk to my friend. He went over to the monastery, found the monk, and delivered him to my side."

The interruption of the retreat program and the monastic day was not welcome. Father Dan is no different from any of us that way. He does not look forward to having his plans disrupted and having to deal with an additional problem. His lifetime of monastic formation, however, prevented him from ignoring the woman. He felt the same frustration anyone feels when faced with such a situation, but he also knows that moments like these hold the potential for holy presence—and that's not something to hide from. When such a moment presents itself, you run toward it and expect that God will show up.

The Benedictine is not merely gracious; he is available. He does not observe human pain from a distance; he gets up to his elbows in it. He can wait with you while you try to make words. There is a deep, open place in his heart where others can come and go. This is Benedictine hospitality. He does not have to attach himself to every person who passes through this open heart of his, however; he can love them at the moment and let them go on.

We are going to have moments when we want no one to cross the threshold of our lives. We are going to experience, at our best, the urge to bolt and run. It helps to know that this happens to the most caring of persons; it happens to the monk. Hospitality calls us to push past those feelings and extend ourselves.

Hospitality enables you to joyfully make room for another inside your open heart. It stretches the brittle, tight heart. A closed-up heart can never relax, never allow you to enjoy another, to play, to relish the unguarded moment of surprise. It is always waiting for the other person to strike.

Only the secure person can live with an open heart. To do so is a whole lot braver than it sounds. You become susceptible to all sorts of human oddities and strangeness. You will be misunderstood. You will be rejected. Doubts you could otherwise avoid will circle your feet. You have to resolve the issue of whether or not the universe is a safe place. Only the brave keep the door ajar.

Brave hearts eventually shine with the divine presence; like God they are free, they are welcoming and accepting, they are strong, yet gentle. They are wondrously available. Yes, it will be costly. People will enter your heart and your life; they will become precious to you and then they will leave. An open heart will be broken. This is all undeniable.

But, by remaining open we learn about ourselves and we grow in ways we'd never otherwise grow. We discover why it is hard for us to trust and love. We encounter the broken places we have ignored; we listen to the voices of our deepest longings to connect. We pay attention to distinctions. We learn the sound of a malicious lie and learn to discern it from the whisper of a frightened one. Discernment, a vital element in wisdom, grows in those who remain open, despite the high cost.

As the practice of hospitality increases our wisdom and openness, we tend to become more aware of the deeper implications of hospitality. We come to recognize that the need for hospitality goes deeper than we originally realized. Pursuing a life of hospitality will eventually make you realize its social and moral implications. What you do, as one person, to receive others does matter. Hospitality, however, involves us not only as individuals, but also as our entire culture. In a culture that excludes others, prejudice and hatred are common. Prejudice has deeper effects, in addition to simply causing people to exclude others: it is at the root of a hostility that is cruel and violent.

We have made great strides in better understanding one another, but there will be prejudice until you and I deal with our prejudice. There will be sexism until we rip up its roots in our own hearts. Until we take people of other races into our hearts we will not recognize "them" as real human beings. Until we have loved a gay person we will fear a gay person. Until we get to know someone who practices a religion different than our own, our differences will divide us. The walls only come down when the labels are changed into human faces.

When my little girl Gina was four, she went through what the pediatrician called a normal stage of development for her age. She became frightened of sleeping. Understandable if you consider things from her viewpoint. The world she knows changed when she slept. The cute little stuffed bear at the foot of her bed growled in the night and nibbled her toes. The whirl of her ceiling fan might be comforting when sunlight streams through the windows, but at night it casted shadows transforming the security of her room into a threatening jungle.

Gina coped with the trauma of the night by developing a complicated set of rituals to ease her away from the people she loved into the mystery of the night she faced alone. Bedtime helps us learn to face our fears and deal with the unknown. Rituals such as taking the last drink of water, reading five books, and leaving the door open three—not two, not four, but three—inches, gives the child some sense of control over such a frightening thing.

The most important ritual for Gina was having me sit at the edge of her bed while she fell asleep. She ceased the continual requests to go to the bathroom one more time, or get another tissue, or rearrange a shelf of books, if I simply sat with her, put a comforting hand on hers, and stayed with her in the night for a few minutes.

Now, even in the upheaval of impending teen years, Gina has an amazing ability to calm herself. She sinks into the feeling of a loving presence, she pulls it around herself and breathes deeply until her anxieties melt into the night. She does not feel alone in the dark—even when, physically, she is.

What we need as we take steps toward the frightening idea of hospitality is someone to sit with us until it feels more comfortable. We don't need to be judged or scolded for our unsettled feelings and fears. We need a companion in the darkness. Benedict and his monks are our companions in this unknown region. We will not whistle in the dark and pretend to be unafraid, and we will not deny the inherent dangers. Acknowledging fear, facing fear, and sitting with it, this is a spiritual approach to hospitality.

Night Prayer is the way the monks go into the depths of mystery. Night is a sacred time of silence at a monastery. Each monk goes bravely into the night silence alone, and yet his brothers accompany him. If facing the possibility of hospitality can be compared to entering the unknown mystery of night, there is no better companion for the journey into the night than the monk. He knows this region. He has been there. He won't be easily startled by what rattles and chills the night.

In monasticism, the night is a holy time. God is experienced in the darkness in a way that is unique to darkness. And God in the dark makes the frightful thing less so. Fear chokes out love. We don't become people of love unless we have faced our fears. This doesn't always mean we reach resolution. Overcoming fears can be the work of a lifetime.

Hospitality is the way we learn to really love; it is the way out of our own brooding fears and broken hearts. Benedictine hospitality is a far cry from the tame social grace we have come to call hospitality. Hospitality feels risky, but it is the most ordinary of human experiences. In a less complicated world, less painful world, we would not be discussing *how* to open up; we would simply do it.

It is not a comforting thing for the future or our race that we discuss simple human relations as if we are doing quantum physics. Just as a person with a healthy digestive system doesn't talk about it, people with healthy relationships don't make a fuss over it; they just live a certain way. When our lives are working and our spirits are alive, we are mostly unaware of ourselves.

That doesn't mean our interest in how to be more loving and accepting is sick. The interest is normal and healthy, but there is a soul sickness that provokes the discussion. We are not as well adjusted as we think we are. The widespread talk of spirituality in our culture is not encouraging news about the state of our spirits. And this is the place where we must begin. We must go into the places inside of us we avoid. We must take a deep breath, and take a hand, and be brave. Hospitality does not require a new cookbook and tea set. It requires what we used to call conversion.

three

Hospitality Begins Inside

*O*n considering the meaning and ways of hospitality, we are looking for a first step in a new direction. It's natural. It's something we human beings need: a first thing to do, followed by another thing, and then another. How do you begin? It is important to understand that we aren't offering ten easy steps to hospitality. That is not how spiritual practices work.

Well, then, how do spiritual practices work? A spiritual practice is an action intended to make a change or adjustment in the deepest realm of the self. A spiritual practice is a thing we do that opens a door. It might be meditation or prayer. It could be serving the poor. Stripping life of what is unessential and practicing simplicity—that is a spiritual practice. The spiritual practice creates a possibility or opportunity, but the change itself is more gift than effort. The spiritual practice puts us into a receiving place where we are open to the something more that we call God. You can set your will to be more open to others, but your heart still has to stretch gradually.

This description is hard to wrap the mind around when so much of contemporary culture approaches spirituality from a self-help angle. American spirituality is basically consumer spirituality. God is a product with incredible benefits. God helps us live well, live healthfully, be prosperous and emotionally strong. God is like a great motivational speaker or talk show host who offers a banquet of options for successful spirituality. You look over the banquet table and select what appeals to you.

We are caught up in what is probably the most immature attempt at spirituality humanity has ever seen. It is tragically and poignantly adolescent, with the deep emotion and angst that goes with adolescence. It is a spirituality that seeks improvement for life—a better me, a better relationship—but it does not seek God and it does not move us toward others. It seeks benefits rather than relationship. It just keeps us running on the treadmill of our little egocentric worlds.

hospitality begins inside | 71

We are accustomed to easy answers. Hospitality is not an easy answer. It requires that we take a chance and we change. It requires us to grow. The moment we engage with another person, everything gets messy. Our time becomes not quite our own; we can count on others interrupting us. We become subject to a whole hoard of emotional dangers. Because hospitality always involves giving something of ourselves to others, it is a spiritual practice. Spirituality is about relationship. When you and I become confused about the meaning of spirituality, remembering that spirituality is about relationship will bring us back to the basics: relationships.

If you receive many mail order catalogs, you have noticed that common household items and clothing are now sold with a spiritual promise. Turn on your soothing music, wrap up in your cotton robe, curl up beneath a silk and wool afghan, light a candle, and plug in your flowing fountain. The ads suggest that you should now be feeling spiritual. And it cost you only a couple hundred dollars.

What we want in spirituality today is comfort. Tom Waite and Kathleen Brennan wrote a song called "Chocolate Jesus." It's about wanting a Jesus that tastes good, gives you the comforts of sweets and fast food, and makes you feel tingly—a Jesus as sweet and comforting as chocolate. A chocolate Jesus to "make me feel good inside."

Americans want chocolate spirituality that soothes and feels good. We think it is "good enough for me," but it isn't; it's not good enough for anyone. Genuine spirituality is not cozy and seldom makes you comfortable. It challenges, disturbs, unsettles, and leaves you feeling like someone is at the center of your existence on a major remodeling mission. While affirming how wonderful you are, better than you really know, spirituality is also meant to change you. If it doesn't, it is something less than spirituality. This tendency of ours to seek out comfort should tell us something about ourselves. We lack. We need.

We sense something is not quite right. But Chocolate Jesus and chicken soup don't help the problem. We need stronger medicine for our sickly souls. We need a transforming, shake-you-to-the-soles-of-your-feet kind of remedy. We need transforming love. You want to be open, you want to let others into your life— what do you do? Whatever plan you devise, one thing is undeniable: such a change starts within. It begins with who you are and who you are becoming. It is a spiritual journey.

I recall receiving an e-mail from a student in Indonesia who had read some of my books. In his correspondence he said very gracious things and at the end he wrote, "May I know you better?"

Here is the core of hospitality: May I know you better? Will you come closer, please? No, it will not be easy, but make no mistake about it: your life depends on this saving stranger coming to you and stretching your tight little heart.

Hospitality is a personal response to your own need to connect with other people. This need is at the core of what it means to be human. Your entire humanity, your identity itself, is wrapped up in your need to connect. The real question is not how dangerous that stranger is. The real question is how dangerous will I become if I don't learn to be more open?

Choosing against hospitality means you will eventually lock your heart away from others and grow cold and hard inside. You cannot take seriously the spiritual practice of hospitality and remain as you are. If you are serious about it, nothing will ever be the same again.

A few years ago, the J.R.R. Tolkien classic *The Lord of the Rings* gained popularity as a movie based on the books. The books are the story of one person's (well, one hobbit's) resistance to evil and his mission in life to stop the invasion of evil. Along the way he finds companions and they, too, are forced to make decisions about the kind of people they will be and what they will spend their lives for.

The hobbit is an interesting character because he is considered by most to be not quite human, a "halfling"—part human, part animal (he is small and has animal-like feet that never require shoes or boots). He does not try to be anything other than what he is, he lives at peace with this in-between state of his, and he does what he is given to do. The message is a simple one. We are, none of us, as human as we might be. We are all still part animal. This mixed bag is our reality, but it does not prevent us from doing the great and good things we are given to do.

At one point the hobbit sets out to fight evil on his own but discovers, in the movie, that he cannot get rid of his companions. Nuisance and hard to understand though they may sometimes be, they are part of whatever plan exists in our universe. They are part of the struggle against not only the darkness in our universe, but the darkness inside as well. We are in this together.

Hospitality, rather than being something you achieve, is something you enter. It is an adventure that takes you where you never dreamed of going. It is not something you do, as much as it is someone you become. You try and you fail. You try again. You make room for one person at a time, you give one chance at a time, and each of these choices of the heart stretches your ability to receive others. This is how we grow more hospitable—by welcoming one person when the opportunity is given to you.

The other day over lunch I overheard an interesting conversation. Two couples, both in their forties, were discussing matters such as Sunday school classes and how to talk to others about faith. In the middle of the conversation one man in the group told the story of going to a huge march in Washington several years ago with a million other men, all in the name of Christian faith. He talked about how their walking route was "littered with the homeless and people begging." One of his friends obviously was struggling with his feeling that they should have stopped to help these people. The others in the group discouraged him from such thoughts by saying, "Hey, they've made their choice. No one is making them do this. They could get a job."

In their conversation they wondered about what to do in these situations. As they talked, a fear surfaced.

"Yeah, we know we're supposed to help people, but what if this is what they do for a living? I mean, what if they go drive a Mercedes home at the end of the day?"

Maybe they really are not poor. Maybe they are ripping me off. What if they are getting what they deserve? What if God wants them to be poor? They have made their own choices. There are programs to help people like them. I am not doing them a favor if I give them a handout. I am not going to contribute to their condition.

We have all heard that voice rattling around in our heads. They were people like us wrestling with the same kinds of things you and I leave unsaid day after day.

There are no easy answers. Benedict offers none except that we must be open to others, *especially*, he says, to the poor and the outcast. Benedict was Christian and so Jesus was his model for how to treat the poor.

Jesus told his followers: If you ignore them, you ignore me. If you feed them, you feed me. So, Benedict tells his monks, receive every person as if you are receiving Christ himself. Simple statement. Huge goal.

The foursome appeared to be honestly grappling with the issue; you could not doubt their sincerity. They wrestled with these issues because they are people of faith and Jesus gave Christians only one option. You help when you can help. Give what you have. The resolution to the big problem is somehow, mysteriously, wrapped up in this uniquely Christian notion that Jesus is in the poor. When we turn away from the poor, we lose Jesus and we lose ourselves.

We can't know how our behavior changes everything, but it does. We call that faith. It was not Washington's homeless those good Christian men walked past, but Jesus.

Daily, Benedict tells his monks, you and I will encounter Jesus. You will stroll right past him if you aren't careful. Instead, look closer, look in the person's eyes, search for that spark of light, and let yourself be open to the possibility of God coming to you in the stranger.

In most situations we get ourselves into trouble by what we do: adultery, lying, stealing, jealousy, and so on. Not so in hospitality: our error comes through what we fail to do. When it comes to hospitality we become less by what we omit doing. Every time we turn away we drop a little of our humanity.

The point is not even whether or not you change the world by putting a dollar in the hand of one hungry person. The point is that you be open. Anyone can give a few dollars today, anyone can take someone for a cup of coffee, anyone can drop a blanket around someone's shoulders.

These are little acts, to be sure, but little acts push at the great big darkness, the darkness that is so huge we feel helpless and so we do nothing and then try to make ourselves feel good about it. This is a heart problem. We don't lack resources or opportunity, we lack heart. You can't fix the problem of world hunger. Well, no, of course you can't. Where did you ever get the idea you were supposed to? But you can help the single mother feed her kids, and you can help the old guy whose Social Security check won't come for another week. You and I, we can help the one in our path. That is enough. Try to get this straight—that really is enough.

Imagine that all of life is a great symphony. You play the violin. That is what you are good at, what you love, what you were made to do. So play it. Become really good at playing your notes, and just your sound can be incredible, but you will not be the whole symphony. The symphony requires all the other musicians.

But the violinist must play her notes if the symphony is to be the wonder it is and is supposed to be. She is neither the whole symphony nor insignificant.

We read books, listen to speakers, talk to the older and wiser, hoping that they will offer some method, some path toward becoming more loving. We want someone to give us the next step. Hospitality is not a self-improvement goal to be achieved, such as giving up smoking. Hospitality is not about what you do; it is about who you are becoming. You can press the linens, invite the homeless, and serve the ham. But unless you are willing to let people into your locked-up secret place you will remain alone and so will they. This becoming tends to be subtle rather than startling. It starts with a choice to begin. That is how all change starts: you decide it is time to change.

Somewhere, sometime you will be presented with a choice. You can listen to the old woman and be ten minutes late for your meeting or you can rush her, maybe even ignore her—and be admirably prompt. You can put down the phone and listen to your coworker talk for a minute. You can shut off the radio and play checkers with your child. A healthy practice of hospitality means finding a healthy balance. It is about priorities as well as the state of your heart. How much do people matter? How important is it to make room for others?

Just the other day one of the retreat staff at St. Benedict's was telling a handyman about the needs of one special teenager who has been on retreat a couple of times. "She's a wonderful girl," he told the handyman. "I'm not sure what her physical impairment is, but she is weaker on one side than the other." He instructed the handyman to install handrails in the bathroom and shower of the room where the girl would be staying. One girl. Thousands of teens will make a retreat at the monastery this year, but the monks were willing to make room for one girl.

That is where it starts. You make room in your heart, room in your life, room in the moment for one person, with no strings attached.

All your life someone has been reminding you not to talk to strangers. All of these well-meaning people only wanted to protect you when you were a child. You are not a child any longer; it is time for you to determine how you will respond to the strangers among us. What is dangerous to the child is not dangerous to an adult. You drive a car now. You live away from home. You use knives to chop vegetables. You drink a scotch and water. Why do we remain locked up in our fear of strangers?

Sharon, a thirty-something-year-old woman from a small Midwestern town, was on a committee formed to consider establishing a homeless center in conjunction with an established center in a nearby troubled city. The inner-city shelter housed more men than they could handle each night. In someone's will, the shelter had been given a large, well-built home in Sharon's quiet little town. The plan was to bus the extra men to that home each night and then back to the streets of the city the next day after breakfast. Sharon joined the committee because she assumed they would be helping implement the plans. Imagine how surprised she was to discover that the committee's actual goal was to prevent the homeless shelter from carrying out its plan. It was her first exposure to, "Yes, they need help, but not in our neighborhood," and, "Our streets won't be safe with those people here," and, "Homeless people are always a little nuts, you know."

Sharon knew she could not turn around the attitude of the committee. She chose to inform the shelter of the committee's true intention. She held out no hopes that her decision to inform would make a difference—and she was right. Ultimately the shelter sold the house and used the money to purchase and restore a building in the city. She knew it was a better plan than the original one, but she remained profoundly disturbed by what she had heard.

"It was such an awful thing they were doing to people they don't know. I'm not saying I never feel prejudice—but they would not even give the homeless a chance." The others ostracized Sharon, including several who went to church with her. To this day there are people who still call her "that woman." However, Sharon has continued to grow and let her heart be open to others. She lost friends, but she gained an open heart.

Hospitality means sharing. What a wildly quaint idea. We reserve the word *sharing* for toddlers these days. Hospitality allows us to grow into the human family and share space, materials, resources, and ourselves. The other option is to remain locked up in our little neighborhoods, frightened that someone different might sneak in. When I begin to realize that I am one among many, I begin to realize that someone else is real. Someone else has a right to space, too. Someone else has needs. Someone else has as much right to be here as I do. I am not more. I am not less. I am part of it all.

The work of opening up to others can be challenging. For most, there are more than a few personal barriers to overcome. We fear bonding and we fear detachment, and we seldom know how to strike a healthy balance between them. Growing more open is easier if we don't understand these twin realities as polar opposites. The need to belong and the need to be alone are both normal and do not exclude the other.

There are other problems: We may bond too quickly and too possessively. We may smother others with what we want to give them. No matter how much we want to know someone better and be present to him or her, we must not be obsessive and overwhelming. We need to stand back and let people find their way to our open hearts.

Brenda once attempted to develop a close friendship with a woman who prided herself on being "open and honest" with everyone.

"Her idea of honesty was brutal. She said things like, 'You're much smarter than your wife. Why are you married to such a dimwit?' Or, 'Your father died because he smoked three packs of cigarettes a day.'

"She immediately wanted into your psyche, she wanted instant access to all your deepest regions and would get very upset when people didn't 'open up' to her. She considered it a deep fault. She was so bent on pushing you into being open and honest, that you didn't want her nearby."

Brenda watched her friend push away person after person, all the while blaming the others. It came to a head when a neighbor of Brenda's was hospitalized with a nervous breakdown, and her three children needed care and supervision.

"She was the first one to volunteer her help and support. I admired that. When it came time for her to stay overnight with the children (their father worked nights) she asked me to drive her because her car was in the shop. We arrived just as the children's father was getting ready for work. After a couple minutes of small talk my friend said, 'What your wife needs is more love from you. You've failed as a husband or she wouldn't be in the hospital.' The young man was devastated. Those who knew the history knew the woman had been engaged in a struggle for her emotional health since her teens."

Brenda was furious with her friend. She could not believe that even this woman would say such a thing. Brenda decided she would also stay the night with the children. After the children were in bed she tried to talk about what had happened.

"As soon as I brought it up she left the room to make tea. I brought it up again and she became angry. She said that no one understood this was her gift and God had given her the responsibility of speaking the hard truth."

The friendship faded slowly, Brenda remembers. "If that was a gift of God, it was one I didn't understand, one that seemed unusually cruel and selfish. I tried to find the better part of her and that was easy; there was a lot to like. But in the moments when she turned on a person, it was so fierce. I chose not to put myself through that over and over again. What I learned in that relationship was to honor myself and make better choices in my relationships. I could have remained friends with her, but it was too costly to my peace of mind. I tried the best I knew, and then I allowed the relationship to die."

Part of the internal work hospitality requires is setting boundaries. You do no one a favor if you allow people to involve you in destructive behaviors. You have to figure out for yourself when this is happening. It is a matter of trusting yourself.

You can be accepting with people without trying to make everyone your best friend. It is not even healthy to try to be intimate with everyone. I will address this more later when discussing intimacy in more detail. For now, keep in mind that hospitality requires a healthy set of personal boundaries you do not allow others to violate.

The paradox of relationship is that we will never achieve any better relationship with anyone else than we have achieved with ourselves. If you genuinely open up to others you will be unable to ignore all the stirrings inside of you, all the unresolved questions, and all the still-weeping wounds. You will be forced to look deeper into yourself. Others help us understand ourselves in all the annoyance, bewilderment, and companionship of relationship.

There is a kind of gentle hospitality with the self that most of us fail to practice. You know that moment you look in a mirror and see a stranger staring out those eyes? We don't accept the stranger within. We dread the regions of ourselves we don't understand. By learning to value the otherliness of the actual stranger, we honor the mystery within us, too.

The stranger in your house is not just yourself; it is your teenager or spouse or brother. Not only is there a stranger in your skin, there are several in your home too. The essence of hospitality is receiving the stranger while letting them remain a stranger. By letting the stranger into our "dwelling" (not necessarily a physical structure), we let them into our emotional and spiritual space. We welcome them to be heard and understood, we accept what they choose to reveal of themselves, and we accept them if they reveal little or nothing.

We've all been shocked by some hidden aspect of someone we have known and loved, or by some part of ourselves that suddenly reveals itself. It can be disturbing, yet we see the person in a new light, we pay closer attention, we ask questions, we cease taking them for granted and assuming we have mined the depths.

There is a value in the unknowing between people. Extending hospitality to the people we know means that we allow them freedom to make mistakes. It means we give them room to be who they are, rather than who we want them to be.

The mystery of the other is a reflection of God's mystery as well. God is ultimately the stranger who comes to us, the stranger within, the stranger who intrudes with her neediness and her hurting. God is the stranger we never quite understand.

I recall going to Father Dan when I was very disturbed over the behavior of a mutual acquaintance. I was surprised to learn that Dan had also struggled to understand and accept that particular individual. Dan's monastic training meant he tried extra hard to listen between the lines; he tried extra hard to find the good in this person even when the person was being a jerk.

"What is the secret to your patience?" I asked. He shrugged his shoulders and said, "There's no secret to it, you just keep trying to understand."

We need patience, with others and with ourselves, if we are going to live hospitable lives. If we are impatient we invade other people and violate their sacred rights. Patience allows others to approach us as they feel welcome. Patience gives space. We become receptive to new ideas, to good criticism, to encouragement, to change.

A teenager told me how she discovered her own lack of patience. She was babysitting for the children across the street. Michael, a boy of three, resisted even what was good for him. He did not want to eat. He did not want to sleep. He did not want to share with his sister. He did not want a bath. He did not want to put his pajamas on over his head; he wanted them pulled up over his feet. An experienced sitter, she knew there is nothing unusual about a strong-willed toddler, so her reaction to Michael surprised her.

"I wanted to hurl him out a window," she remembers. "I wanted to force the food down his throat and I wanted to tie him to his bed. The entire evening this terrible sense of violence was just under the surface. I had no patience for the child, none at all."

The girl said when she talked to her mother, she realized that it was a control issue. Her inability to control the child or bend him to her will broke whatever reserves of patience she had. "Impatience is the offspring of the need to control," writes James

Connor in his book *Silent Fire: Bringing the Spirituality of Silence to Everyday Life*.

We all experience frustration with others on a nearly daily basis: The friend who stops in without calling. The spouse who returns your car with the gasoline tank on empty. The coworker who holds up a project by missing a deadline. We cannot make them stop it. We cannot make them behave in a way that is convenient and acceptable. Like the babysitter, we want to hurl them out a window.

We can begin by listening to the sound of our need to control rather than accept.

Hospitality may involve a major change of attitude and lifestyle for you, or it may be that you are already growing more open to others. But either way you will sometimes find it easy to welcome others, while at other times you will fight for every ounce of acceptance you offer. A battle to accept someone can seem like a struggle with no real value. Remind yourself that the struggle matters—it is making you stronger.

I have a friend who owns a sculpture of a horse in the grips of an exerting struggle. It is a stunning sculpture: the dark form of the horse almost writhes in the agony of some huge unknown effort. Even after looking at it for hours, you cannot determine if the horse is falling down or getting up. You only see the exertion. My friend says she changes her mind from day to day as to whether the horse is getting up or falling down. She says it seems to depend on what she is feeling that day. When she mentioned this to the artist, he said, "You know, it doesn't matter if the horse is falling down or getting up. What matters is it keeps trying."

In our relationships with others what matters is that we keep trying. There is a place inside that you must first open, before you open your door. Some days it will be hard to do that; other days it will be easier. What matters is that you keep trying.

four

Welcoming the Other

He was from Saudi Arabia, and if he sat next to you on a bus he'd make you nervous. I didn't meet him on the bus. I met him, his wife, and their two children while working as a volunteer at a refugee center, in a program run by the monastery that involves service projects by teens and adults. This particular project was slated to last only a few days, possibly a week.

I met him while painting rooms on the floor where they lived. He had just returned from a visit to the library, he said. We talked a little. Despite his best efforts, his English was poor. That day we managed to exchange names. He told me his wife's name and the names of his children, a boy and a girl, both under six. He asked why I was painting rooms at the shelter. How did I know all the teenagers with me? Were any my own children?

He listened to me speak with apparent interest. It was something more than listening. He repeated certain words. He watched my mouth move when I spoke and leaned in to hear better. While speaking, he would often stop and ask if he was using the words correctly.

The conversation lasted about twenty minutes. He joined his family and I returned to painting.

The next day he came looking for me while I painted on another floor. He asked, "Will you meet my family?" He had told his wife about me. She missed having women to speak with, missed the sound of her mother's voice.

To say that I was conflicted does not begin to describe my feelings. He was different from any person I had ever known. He was Muslim. My head buzzed with everything I had ever heard about Muslims, especially Muslim men. But I liked his wife immediately. She had a wide smile and a soft voice. She had been in medical school and hoped to return some day. She was an intelligent woman trying to make the best of a terrible situation. Her soft laughter, the warmth in her eyes—she had me almost immediately.

I noticed the tenderness between the couple in small gestures, glances, and smiles. Their behavior was different than I expected. I could not have put it into words at the time, but something about them and their lovely little ones touched me deeply. Their children were delightful, nothing like any child I expected to find in a refugee center.

Their father asked the children to tell me something about a museum they had visited a few days before. They each did, carefully and slowly. The wife asked if the children were using the words correctly. They were, remarkably so, I replied, and the parents beamed with pride.

That night, I lay awake wondering about the mysterious man and his family. I mentally went through the numerous stereotypes I carried around about Muslim families. It was disturbing to have the stereotypes so blatantly revealed. Still, I reminded myself, the man was a mystery. We were given no information about the guests at the center, but we knew they were often fleeing for their lives. What had he done?

Mystery surrounds all human relationships, but especially a relationship with a stranger. This man was clearly accustomed to holding power. He carried himself like royalty, as did his whole family. His cheerfulness bewildered me. I had spent very little time with him, but still, he had been cheerful without exception. There he was, dislocated from the only life he had ever known, and the man bubbled with hope and optimism.

I went home that evening wondering about his motivations, asking myself what it was he wanted from me. He made me feel uneasy, not because of anything he did but because he was very different from any other person I had ever known. I thought Muslims disliked Christians. I thought Muslim men did not like or respect women. He had exploded the preconceptions of my clenched little heart in only a few hours.

The next day he was waiting when I pulled into the parking lot with a van of teenagers. He asked if we could speak in private. I told one of the other adults where I'd be and then walked next door and sat on the steps of he church.

We drank coffee and he told me his story. He was a political refugee. His crime was resistance to what he considered rigid and evil political systems. He had been involved in lawmaking. He came from a prosperous family that owned more than one house. He talked of moving his bride into a twenty-four room house when they married.

"It breaks my heart that she is making a home of a little room now," he said, lifting his eyes toward the center. "Her courage is so big that I will do all to give her a better life now."

He was not sure how long he would be in America; there were rumors that they would soon be moved to Canada. He understood his present situation to be an opportunity, a gift of God. It was not a tragedy. He expected their life would be better, his children better, because they would grow up in the Western world.

He was at peace despite having left everything he had ever known. Despite being marked for assassination. Despite facing changes that would leave most people staggering, bitter, and frightened, he was at peace.

He said with conviction that Allah had sent me to his family to teach them "better English." He had watched me, he said, and noticed that I worked hard and treated others kindly. He was not sure, but he thought my English was above average. Would I teach him, and his family, about America? Would I help them improve their English? "There is nothing to give you in return, but we will give gratitude," he said.

I did not know what to say. I was not sure such a thing would be allowed by the center. They were very protective of the residents. I told him we'd need permission from the program director.

He was disappointed that I did not immediately agree and we could not get started on the spot. My real problem was not whether or not I would be allowed to help. He still made me uneasy. I could not imagine having anything to offer them, either. They were so different. They made me hugely uncomfortable.

I had become a good friend of the monks by this time. Observing their lives, listening to them talk, reading St. Benedict, I believed helping them was the right thing to do. But it was also the difficult thing to do. I didn't realize until I talked to the program director just how difficult.

Yes, I could "tutor" the family, the director said, but I could not tell them my full name, where I was from, or discuss my family. In fact, the less they knew about me the better. "Do not give them your phone number," the director ordered, "or your address." They could not tell me any more about themselves than they had already (and the director was *not* pleased with what they had already revealed). She said that when the family was relocated to their final destination, there could be no more contact between us. Did I understand the seriousness of their situation—that their lives were at stake? Well, I did after that talk.

Strengthened by my blossoming understanding of Benedictine hospitality, I hesitatingly agreed to help the family. For the next six weeks I spent two afternoons a week with the Muslim family.

Before long I started looking forward to our time together. The tutoring sessions were nothing like I expected. We talked and we read newspapers together, we went to movies or museums. We visited the zoo. I read book excerpts to them sometimes. I told them stories of growing up in Middle America and being Catholic. We went from a tutor/student relationship to a friendship.

I shed my assumptions about Muslims in those weeks, not because I am by nature without prejudice, but because the mysterious Muslim now had a face—a laughing face with bright, dark eyes and a friendly welcome for me. I had taken on the task of teaching them about American culture, but they were doing something much more important for me. They were dismantling my ignorance, my fears, and my prejudices.

One afternoon, I took the children to a Disney movie, leaving their parents to some rare time by themselves. I sat between the children, anticipating the need to explain the movie. But the music and the characters—it was all so universal and simple. They didn't understand line by line, yet they laughed a lot and bounced to the songs and ate bags of popcorn and drank gallons of lemonade. At one point during the movie, the little girl rested her head sleepily on my shoulder and smiled up at me in the dim lights. It was such a common gesture of trust. My own children had done the same hundreds of times. It said, "I trust you and I feel safe with you."

On the way home that day I taught them to sing "The Wheels on the Bus." When I left the children, they were teaching it to their parents amidst silly gestures and lots of laughter.

When I showed up two days later they were gone. The director explained they had started their new life. She handed over a piece of blue scrap paper, folded in half. It said: "Thank you for considerations to us. You are a good woman and Christian. May Allah be with you all the days of your life and reward you for kindness to strangers." I couldn't take the note home with me. The director would destroy it after I left that day.

My friend was keeping his word and "giving gratitude." We would never say good-bye. I would never tell him that they had given me so much more than I gave them. They had opened up a place inside of me, filled it with friendship and trust, banishing some particularly fearsome things from my heart. They had taught me to love better.

I felt the loss of my new friends deeply. I still think of them sometimes and pray they are safe, happy, and free. They are the face of the Muslim faith for me. When I am tempted to buy into the stereotypes—I see their faces and I remember.

You may recall a popular song by Joan Osborne titled "One of Us." It asked, "What if God was one of us, just a stranger on the bus, trying to make his way home?"

That is what Christians believe Jesus showed us about God—that God is one of us and is with us as we try to get home. God came to us to teach us how to live and how to love. One of the things he said, "Whatever you do to the least of my brothers and sisters, you do to me," means that God *is* the stranger on the bus. We are all strangers on the bus of this world trying to make our way home.

We welcome strangers in the little ways we open ourselves up to them. Let's consider what it means to be the "other." The other is the one who is not like me. She is the liberal if I am conservative, the rich if I am poor. He is the guy who does not go to the same places I go, the family that does not worship where I worship or shop where I shop. The other is the person from the neighborhood I avoid, the woman I don't want sitting next to me on the plane. He is the person who votes for the candidate I consider way off the mark.

When Father Dan needs rest and rejuvenation he sometimes takes a break at a small cottage on a lake in Ontario. Near the cottage is a little gas station where he buys a few groceries and picks up a daily newspaper. He noticed they also rented a few movies.

One day, Dan went into the gas station for his loaf of bread and newspaper. He noticed the videos were gone. When he asked the owner about it, making small talk, the man flew into a rage about the migrant workers. He called them all thieves, lumping them all under one label and demeaning the whole bunch. You have probably heard similar things.

What we notice most about the "other" is how much he or she is not like me. Most of us don't respond with the kind of vehemence of the store owner. At least not out loud. Our negative opinion of strangers is usually a little quieter. We do not intentionally put people at a distance, but we can't help but notice that there are some who are not like me. This unlike-me-ness disturbs us for reasons that seem almost instinctive.

Could it be that as a culture we are covertly indoctrinated to mistrust the stranger? Could it be so common that we consider it normal? We tend to surround ourselves with people who agree with us, look and smell like us, have similar backgrounds and hold similar convictions. It's natural isn't it? Natural. Normal. Pretty powerful concepts.

Our closest relationships are built on what we share and have in common. We build relationships at work, school, church, and in our neighborhoods. We meet people while we serve on the board of some local charity or in a service club. Thus we form a social sphere of people who are like us and do not feel like actual strangers. The problem with this manner of forming relationships is that we may exclude those who are not like us. We don't exclude them intentionally, but our worlds tend to be small and homogenous. We don't go looking to be made uncomfortable. That would be, well . . . unnatural.

But, let's consider the possibility that what we consider "natural" and "normal" is upside down. It brings us to a concept we seldom speak of: original sin. The theology of original sin varies in details—even among Christians. I stand among those who believe that original sin doesn't mean people are innately evil, but rather that we originate in a toxic, fallen world that has gone wrong through human choices. We are not responsible for the choices of those who have gone before us, but we are stuck in the world and culture of their ruined legacy.

In such a world, something could feel "natural" when it is infected and dangerous to our souls and our lives together. How often do we hear the person who ends a marriage declare that it "felt right" to abandon their family for selfish pursuits? In a world like ours, we are wise to question what feels "right" when it smacks of self-serving.

As a spiritual discipline, Benedict understood the importance of encountering those who are different from ourselves because it stretches us; it dislocates stiffness and opens us up to new possibilities. He meant for the monks to do so intentionally. Monks are not to take sin lightly.

Sin is whatever you do that pushes away others and God (if you believe in God); if you don't believe in God, you're likely to consider something a "sin" if it harms others or alienates us from the world, culture, or nature. Either way, we understand, on some level, that we ought to be considerate of others and our world.

When we create a life surrounded by people just like ourselves, it is a very narrow life. A spirituality centered in such a life will drift into laziness and complacency. It is the kind of life that allows us to settle for easy answers based solely on personal experience. Letting ourselves believe that our experience constitutes normality and that other ways of doing life are abnormal is delusional and dangerous.

My husband, David, and I are raising our granddaughter Gina as our own child. Gina was four when the first edition of this book was published. She is thirteen now. People my age often look upon us with misguided sympathy. It happened once at a dinner party. A very nice woman suggested that it must be hard raising a child at this stage of our lives.

"You're to be admired for taking your family obligation so seriously when you could be enjoying your middle years instead. . . ."

Hard? Loving Gina, watching her grow, enjoying every moment of every day? She's a gift to us. A delight. A wonder. Hard? No, it isn't hard. We cherish each and every moment we have with her. I stood toe-to-toe with this gracious woman, baffled that anyone would consider such a thing an obligation or a hardship.

I explained that among the grandparents I know in similar situations, most would say the same: the opportunity to raise a grandchild, while complicated and sometimes painful, is overwhelmingly a joy for which they thank God every day.

"We are grateful for Gina. She has never been a burden, and we count every day with her as a divine gift," I said.

The woman who was talking tilted her head and gazed at me as if I were an alien. How could that be? The question hung suspended in the air between us. It seemed we were unintelligible to one another. The woman only knew what she would feel, and she assumed that it was the normal way to feel. She assumed it was how any reasonable person in that situation would feel. It seemed normal to her, and she had thought, at least before the conversation, that I was normal.

But I didn't feel the way she had assigned to me. Not a twinge or a molecule of such thoughts had ever passed through me. It is all simply gift: every breath the child takes, every running through the room and singing of childish songs, every goodnight, every tear, every giggle. I caught my breath the first time I watched her curl her toes into the sand and walk on God's good earth. Every teen crush, every worry over algebra, every single moment upon moment is gift.

As we talked, we saw how our experiences had shaped our attitudes. I have buried three of my five daughters as infants. You do not put tiny caskets into the ground without being changed. Of course I'm aware that every child is a gift and every moment we have with them is a sacred trust. They don't belong to us; they are God's; they are their own. The sick child and the well child, the lovely child and the homely child. None could ever be a burden. God honors us with every gift of every child.

The other woman's experience was different. She had attempted to raise a son, teach school, and do the right thing by her son as a single mother. It had been a struggle, and she had denied herself many things. "Many things," the woman said, sighing deeply. "He will never know what I gave up for him." She loved her son but had not resolved the inner tension of her sacrifices.

In telling me her story the woman said, "It's hard not to resent what I gave up." Before hearing my story the woman had assumed that there is one way to react in such a situation, and that one way is the way *she* would feel.

The woman was not an awful person; she was a retired teacher, very involved with her community, a gracious woman. She had never considered that her ideas were anything other than normal. But such assumptions keep our world small. It never even occurred to her that a person she considers "normal," of her own class, race, and religion, would think or feel differently.

The roles were reversed a few days later when an old friend, Clara, someone I had not heard from in several years, called. Clara's roommate of eleven years had died and Clara was planning to relocate to Arizona. Clara had lived in the top half of her house and her roommate Charles had lived in the lower half. Charles and Clara were longtime friends. Charles was an alcoholic, which Clara knew when she agreed to let him move in. For most of those eleven years, Charles had been a model roommate and a good friend. But in the last three years, the alcoholism had caused brain damage. Charles had needed someone to care for him. So Clara did. She hired help to assist her, but Clara still took most of the responsibility for feeding him and changing his bed and playing cards with him on his better days.

In response to Clara's news, I compassionately replied, "I'm so sorry to hear you lost your friend. It must be a terrible loss. Is there anything I can do?"

Clara, always blunt, said, "Terrible loss? Oh honey, you don't understand, do you? I loved my friend, but his sickness kept me tied to him long after I would have asked him to leave if he had not been sick. Sure, I'll miss the Charles I knew once. I've missed him for a long time, even when Charles was alive. Now, I feel free for the first time in three years."

Hospitality means we don't tell people how to feel. We listen to them. We let them tell us how they feel. This is not easy for a compassionate person to do. We stir up the pot of our own emotion and experience, and the result is what *I* feel. How *I* would respond. How *I* would behave.

When someone dies, we naturally feel compassion for the loss. When we hear that someone's children have made choices that seem painful for the parents, we assume the parent is suffering. These are not negative assumptions. But, in relating to the person, we must offer them room to feel what they feel, rather than assuming that we know what they feel. Even if we think that we have been through exactly the same experience ourselves, we cannot know what another is feeling.

Every person brings to an event their unique history and personality. You can assume that every parent who loses a child in an auto accident is grieving, but you can't know what that grief feels like for the parent.

You only know if you offer an open space in yourself for them to pour out their feelings.

If we consider the possibility that others do not feel and think the same as we do, we suddenly feel very small in a mysterious, expansive universe. There is security in a world where all the others are like me. It's a false security, but we prefer it to no security at all.

When we hold tightly to a worldview in which our own experience is at the center, we live small lives. If we don't consider the ramifications of such a life we can easily slip into suspicion, misunderstanding, and prejudice of strangers—those who do not meet our standard of "normal."

Recently, a friend underwent surgery on her foot. As a result she could not bear weight on it for many weeks. After recovering from surgery enough to drive, she packed her wheelchair and crutches into her Jeep and headed up to a cabin in the woods for some rest. When she arrived at the cabin, alone, a young man was reading the electric meter.

She had planned, on arrival, to call the neighbor (who was expecting her call) for assistance in carrying everything into the house. Instead, the very nice young man helped carry everything into the house, parked her car in the garage, and offered to help unpack and take upstairs anything that needed to go there. When she called her husband to tell him she had arrived, she also mentioned the meter reader and how helpful and gracious he had been.

Her husband replied, "Yeah, we'll see if he was really being nice, or will he be back tonight after dark?" We have all conditioned ourselves toward suspicion.

Suspicion is one of the enemies of hospitality. Fear is at the core of suspicion. We are all starved for love, yet we are mostly unwilling to trust others to give us what we need. We grow callous and hesitant from the fear, always waiting for the other shoe to drop, ever sure of the next rejection. So, we keep people at a distance with suspicion and fear. We fear not only rejection and harm; we fear being used or trapped by love. We fear we will give too much of ourselves and receive nothing or little in return.

Another enemy of hospitality is narcissism. When we place the great "I" at the center of our universe, we give no value to anyone else. We make commodities of people, consuming them for our personal enrichment and happiness. It's common in our culture. The other's only purpose is what he or she can do for us. For many, the only thing that matters is what works for them. There is a kind of contempt in this utilitarian view of others.

You may remember the classic Disney movie *Pete's Dragon* starring Helen Reddy and Mickey Rooney. We watched it dozens of times at our house because Gina loved the movie. It is the story of an orphaned boy, sold into slavery, who has an invisible dragon as a companion. In one scene the townspeople, mostly fishermen, blame the boy because they aren't catching fish. One of them yells, "There's no room here for you."

"There's Room for Everyone" is the song that follows this comment. The lyrics counter the idea that some people don't belong. It's a simple song with a grand idea: move over and share the world.

Hospitality makes room even for the one who is frighteningly different—the dragon, you might say. Hospitality treats people respectfully, as if they are sacred, because they are. Even the other, the stranger, the one who is nothing at all like me. He brings the divine to me, too.

By opening ourselves up to new people, we gain new ideas. We discover the world is filled with people who are nothing like us—and it is a delightful thing. The stranger helps us locate our favorite lies. The stranger helps us see the absurd in our culture and ourselves. The stranger opens our eyes.

Rather than hospitality, however, our culture too often exudes contempt. Our music and movies and television are filled with contempt. Get a life. Been there, done that. Ask me if I care. What part of "no" don't you understand? These little snipes are designed to make one person feel gleefully superior.

One friend told a story of buying magazines at the airport. The girl behind the counter went on to the next customer without giving our friend a bag. Another girl came up from a different part of the store and stood at the counter. Our friend asked for a bag and the girl said, "It's not my shift yet." This is the opposite of hospitality. It is an everyday, happens-much-too-often example of contempt.

Not far from your memory, no doubt, is an image of someone who pulled on big spiked boots and stomped all over your bare soul. It was deliberate. It happens to everyone. That person intended to make you feel small. They refused to make room for you, refused to acknowledge your right to be here.

We tend to remember the childhood offenses, but it happens to adults as well. In places such as grocery stores. I was attempting to move down an aisle so I could get something on my list. Standing in the middle of the aisle was a well-dressed woman with two small children, probably her grandchildren. She looked about seventy. She was selecting a product from the shelves near the bread I was after. The children went to move and let me through. She shot them a paralyzing look and said, "Stay put. I am not finished yet."

Clearly, her stinging words were directed at me, not the intimidated children. It appeared that she perceived others as having no right to share her space. She would not move over and make room on the planet for another. What do you do when faced with such a situation? I glared, reaching for the bread while I held her eyes—because I am not always nice. Then I stewed over it all the way home, muttering and cursing. It ruined my morning.

Benedict would say that you give the woman the space she is demanding. You patiently put up with the crankiness of human nature. When she is finished and moves away, you pick up your bread and you don't lose your peace of mind over it. It is a small way to be hospitable even with a difficult person.

It isn't easy to be open and hospitable when you feel threatened. At the root of many unwelcoming attitudes is fear. If I am not at home in my own skin, enough to let someone share my space, how will I ever be able to look on the stranger with anything like kindness and welcome?

Fear devastates our ability to trust, love, and open up to others. Most of our fears are completely without reason, but not all of them. It *is* reasonable to fear the out-of-control truck barreling down on us. Events and people can actually threaten our lives, threaten what is most important to us. Yet, it is *not* reasonable to fear every stranger or every new idea.

It's not easy to have what we cherish be threatened. In a monastery, the monks live in a certain way. The day unfurls with prayer setting the pace. A monk can count on certain things happening at certain times, and he is pretty sure what face he will see around the next corner.

At least that was so for as long as Brother Benedict could remember. Brother Ben is the oldest member of the St. Benedict Monastery. He's now in his nineties.

He has served the community as cook, and for many years he cared for the cows.

The youth retreat ministry did not involve Ben most of the time. Sometimes when he was up late with a cow who was about to deliver her baby he would run into Father Dan as he passed the retreat house on the way to the barn. That was about it, until the year the monks decided to expand the youth retreat house, making it more comfortable for the kids, while improving the usefulness of the building.

During the building process, Dan and Mary had to take the teens over to the monastery for group projects and meals. Brother Benedict suddenly had teenaged girls in his kitchen. Giggling little girls, tossing their pretty heads and poking into the pots bubbling on the stove. Girls who looked shyly at him as if he were an alien in his own home. This is the kind of thing that can disrupt monastic life.

Ben had a quick smile for the girls. He became quite skilled at teasing the girls and making them laugh. Their presence was profoundly uncomfortable for him, yet he was friendly without exception. These children had overtaken his beloved monastery and his territory—the kitchen—and yet he was called on, by all that is Benedictine, to see in them the presence of the Divine. Hospitality did not allow him to consider them only an inconvenience. He had to find Christ in the mysterious little critters.

So that's what he did. He accepted his current lot in life and tried to enjoy the children who threatened life as he knew it. The girls just loved him. They were always telling Father Dan how much they loved the monk in the kitchen.

A few years later, when the monastery opened up Sunday mass to visitors, there was another period of adjustment, and it would have been natural for the monks to feel that their way of life was threatened again. Even if some of them were wrestling with the decision, they extended a warm welcome to the strangers invading their home and gathered them gently into the monastic family. It was not always easy for the monks, but they soon discovered how visitors and guests enriched the monastic life.

Dan talked about how it felt at the time:

"Looking back over our history, I can see now how two decisions drastically changed our lives as monks: inviting high-schoolers onto our property for retreats beginning in 1975, and welcoming people to our Sunday and daily masses starting in the mid-1990s. In both cases, one would think the welcoming would have been automatic; we are, after all, monks. But it was not a given, because of our unique history."

The monks who founded St. Benedict in 1959 had the vision of the monastery as a novitiate, a place to grow new monks who would then live, love, and minister in the parishes in Detroit. The founding monks had lived monastic life the best they could in parish settings, but they were aware that bustling parishes were not conducive to the growth and development of young monks.

They were not prepared for the new batch of monks to fall in love with the monastic life, outside of a parish setting. Dan was one of those baby monks who first came to St. Benedict's under the fledgling program.

"I was one of a group of young monks who were not interested in serving the parish, except for perhaps a brief time. I wanted to be a monk, a make-a-place-in-the-quiet-and-find-God-in-the-woods kind of monk."

The Benedictine community, Father Dan admitted, stuck with the novitiate perspective for too long. For fifteen years, almost no one other than monks set foot on the monastery grounds. This was unquestioned and considered the status quo.

"It was almost a siege mentality," Dan remembers, "us against them, and if they approached we went into under-siege tactics. There was no malice involved, but it was wrong, and it was not Benedictine."

People would call and ask, "Do you have a mass on Sunday that is open to the public?" The young monks were trained to respond, "Well, yes we do, but our mass is very early and we're hard to find and we are not a parish. Have a blessed day."

The message was clear: stay away. St. Benedict would have throttled the monks.

The ice began to crack in 1975, according to Dan. But, it started earlier when he went away to the University of Toronto to study theology. It was there he first worked with youth. After ordination, the community sent him to serve in their big parish in Detroit.

"It was again against my wishes. Neither Toronto nor Detroit was my idea of a monastic setting."

However, the young monk was growing in his vocation. Benedictine monks are taught to listen. Listen with the heart and not just the ear. What was expected to be one year at the Detroit parish turned into six. During those years, he again worked with youth, and he met the woman who would be his partner in youth retreat work.

"When I finally returned to St. Benedict Monastery in 1975, youth ministry and the normal work of lawn mowing, barn cleaning, and ditch digging were the only kinds of work I knew how to do. So, I proposed to my brother monks that we use a then-unoccupied former barn, which had been remodeled and was presently a library, as a youth retreat house. Okay, the idea had its flaws. There was no dining room, kitchen, conference room, chapel, or much of anything you would need for youth retreats, not even adequate bathroom facilities."

The community was game. After some debate they responded with an overwhelming, "Yes! Let's try it." To date about a hundred thousand teenagers have made a retreat with the Benedictines on the hill in Oxford.

The building was remodeled several years later, then a couple other times, and eventually it tripled in size. They named it Subiaco after St. Benedict's cave. The young people even have used the name of the place to describe the experience itself: "This is my fourth Subiaco. . . ."

The 1975 opening of the monastery to teenagers has affected more lives than can possibly be numbered. When the teenagers walk into Subiaco and look around at the expansive, warm, and beautiful retreat house, they often respond with, "Wow, I can't believe that this is all for us!" You should see their faces when it dawns on them that monks are scrubbing their toilets and showers.

But, opening of the monastery to youth did something for the monks too. Mary Cummings, who helped with the teen retreats from the beginning, became a friend of the community. She was the first nonmonastic to become involved in the life of the community on a regular basis—and a woman. Even crusty old Brother Ben embraced her, because he could see the good she was doing for the monks and the retreat youth. She opened the way for the many who would eventually become friends of the community.

The next opening up of the monastery to strangers happened when the monks moved Sunday mass to a reasonable hour of the morning and allowed the public to attend. It was a huge step.

"When we looked back on all those phone calls and the people we discouraged from coming to mass, we wondered if perhaps those calls were inspired by God to get our attention," says Father Dan.

As you would expect in most monasteries, the majority of monks are introverted by nature. This opening up to outsiders was an enormous mountain they had to climb. Despite the peril, the monks could see something holy was happening among them, and they were determined to increasingly welcome the visitor. Almost all monasteries (including Trappists) are open to the public to some degree, at least on Sundays, but this was new to the monks of St. Benedict Monastery.

They opened the doors and the people came: neighbors, friends, former retreatants and their families, people they had met in parish work, and many, many strangers. All have told the monks, over and over, how grateful they are for the opportunity to celebrate mass with them and share in their life in some small way.

"But we monks know the truth about all this; we are the ones who have received the most from the whole deal," says Father Dan. "We monks were endangered by our isolation. Our identity as Benedictines was threatened because we were disconnected, oblivious to the world beyond our gate. We were professional pray-ers watching from our view on the hill.

"We have discovered that we are grounded in real life in a way that can happen only by encountering real people. It is easy to pray for 'the world' and 'God's people' when you don't have to look into their tear-reddened eyes, or fetch more toilet paper after mass on Sunday. Something sacred and unexpected has happened since we opened our doors and our hearts. Without blurring the line between our monastic family and their families, we have become part of each other's lives."

It is always easier to care for the world, to care for all the others, from a distance. We can even feel good about our prayers for them as long as the people are not in our space and are not taking up emotional space in our hearts. They become harder to handle when they show up and expect something from us. When it gets messy.

The hardest thing about all these people is their absolute otherliness, which cannot be tamed or ignored. They are going to remain unlike us. We are not going to understand them. We should celebrate this. We need them to be different from us. It fits in the way the universe has been designed.

We don't have to make a choice about how we will respond to others, as long as they stay on their side of the fence. In the wilderness of relationships, we contend with powers we'd rather not ever meet up with. We will keep opening the door, and keep making an attempt, and then one night will find us in some holy place and in a holy moment that snatches our breath away.

You will be tucking a child into bed, or pouring a second cup of coffee for your neighbor, or sharing a breadstick with your friend. You will be trying to know what is holy in us all and wondering how to be known by the Holy. You will have read a few books and maybe taken a workshop. You will have spent some time with people reputed to be experts on the subject of hospitality. You will wing it, more often than not.

And then that splinter of light will get through the great mysterious confusion, who knows when or where or why, and grace will sneak up on you and you will know, if only for a splintered flash of a second, you will know that your trying is making a difference and your trying is enough.

On a day like that, all the others you have been trying to let into your weary heart will seem at home in your heart, and like the monks you will know that you and all the others are really part of each other.

five

Cloister, Community, and Hospitality

*C*loister, community, and hospitality: these three together make up a healthy relational ability. They are all tangled together and impossible to separate completely. Hospitality starts at home, after all. And you do not become good at loving the strain of being together in a family or a community if you have not yet learned to be alone.

For purpose of this book, let me clarify, exactly, what I mean by each term. These may not be the only definitions that can be applied to these words. I'm only indicating how the words are going to be used in this chapter.

Cloister refers to the time a monk is alone, or you are alone. It is the apartness of solitude and silence.

Community refers to your closest relationships, the people with whom you share your life. The monk shares life with his community of brother monks. You have friends, family, maybe a spouse or partner.

Hospitality refers to your interactions in all other relationships, especially those outside the security of your comfort zone—relationships with the stranger.

One of the most fascinating things about a monastery is how the monks manage to keep all the facets of their life together in balance. This ability is especially remarkable when some of those facets would appear to be opposites, such as solitude and community. Hospitality can cut into community dynamics. The concepts don't seem to harmonize in all situations.

At the monastery there is always time for prayer, always time to linger with a friend, always time for a needed nap. Work is accomplished as it should be, but in a healthy monastic setting the monks don't obsess over it. The monk has time alone and also time to gather with his community for meals and recreation and meetings.

The triad of *cloister, community,* and *hospitality* represent this balance. These three threads of monastic life weave together to make a strong whole: a whole life and a whole person. Many of us feel we are lacking balance in our lives. We wonder why it is that when life splinters into a million directions we also feel splintered.

In considering the deeper meanings of *cloister, community,* and *hospitality*, we can begin to discern how and where our lives are out of kilter. Are we spending too much time with others and not enough time alone? Are we constantly in social settings and ignoring the most important relationships? Have we isolated ourselves altogether from relationships?

Relationships between monks living in a monastery operate by the same dynamics as your relationships. The monks are a group of men who are committed to going to God together. It is their life together that most profoundly shapes who they become as human beings. Within the monastery, cloister, community, and hospitality represent three states of relating.

Each of these is dependent on the other. They are woven together to create the whole of monastic life. Life outside the monastery is very similar. We need time alone (cloister), we need time with those closest to us (community), and we need to open ourselves to those who are not one of us (hospitality).

The monastic day is purposeful about keeping its holistic balance. The community has time together at prayer, during meals, and in working together and recreation. Silence is a normal part of every monastic day, usually during meals and at other times of the day, such as the silence that begins after Night Prayer and ends after breakfast or Morning Prayer.

Benedict knew the monastery would never be without guests, so he told monks to weave them into their monastic day with reverence and welcome.

Some people, especially those with young children, find it difficult to structure their lives according to this pattern. The trick is to think of it as a pattern and not a model to follow after slavishly. The monastic model simply reminds us to take time for what matters most. Balance your relationships. Take time for those closest to you, be more open to strangers, and do not forget to take time to be alone. We all need regular doses of solitude and silence.

To make this happen, we will need to be intentional about inserting solitude, for example, into our schedules. Most of us cannot long escape our relationships. People who want our attention surround us. The hardest thing can be carving out time for silence. Our contemporary lives are hectic and noisy. We are driven by devices, surrounded by machines. We have grown comfortable with the background noise. How often have you turned on the radio or television just to have the noise, without even thinking about it? Every day you see people driving a car, jogging, reading a newspaper with noise attached to their ears. This does more than keep people at a distance; it keeps life at a distance and also keeps us from noticing what is going on inside us.

Silence is related to solitude. In the monastery there are long periods of silence: meals taken in silence, silent prayer, and hours of solitude. Silence and solitude are related, and we are terrified of them both.

When we are alone, we have cut off our normal routes to escaping ourselves. Not only that, solitude hacks off most of the usual ways we feel affirmed. In solitude we cease being competent workers. We do not serve and nurture others in solitude, and we seldom talk. Once amputated from these normal support systems, we discover a throbbing restlessness that begins to surface.

Thomas Keating, monk and author, calls this the "unloading of the unconscious." What's happening?

Ancient wounds to the psyche begin ascending into the conscious region of the mind. They float up like long-dead bodies. Illusions shatter around us and wisdom gets a chance to get hold of us. If we stick with the process we will know the truth about ourselves. All the glorious truth.

But the bountiful good of the truth does not come until we've danced with a few demons long hidden in the psyche. This is when most people turn on the radio, get in the car, or hustle home to the safety of people, noise, and activity. The purpose of spirituality is not to keep this moment from happening; rather, spirituality will eventually bring it on.

Some people find that in their first experiences of solitude and silence they wrestle with frightful emotions and fantasies. Some dark void in them beckons them to jump over the edge. It does not take long to realize why we avoid ourselves. If you stay with solitude, you discover that this inner void is your friend. It is your true hunger. It has God's name on it. It tells you the truth about yourself, once you are able to push aside all the garbage that initially erupts out of it.

The first stirrings of loneliness, when you are alone, emerge from a vast inner emptiness that can rattle us beyond what we expected. It is then you'll understand what it means to refer to solitude as a state of the mind, rather than a place and time.

We possess inward solitude at a very high cost. It does not come easily. In solitude, we feel helpless and almost out of control. We have grown dependent on others and the noises we make at each other. We do not even know how to imagine our lives without the entire bustle.

A friend of mine asked what I do when I am off somewhere in solitude. She wanted to know what a typical day was like. I explained that I rest. I pray. I might write a little (not related to work, though), go for a walk, weed flowers, fix a simple meal—pray again, or read.

My friend smiled and replied, "Well, okay, that's a morning. What do you do the rest of the time?"

Once, while making a retreat at the monastery, I was staying in the retreat house and had a window cracked open for fresh air. I overheard two monastic novices wondering out loud what I could be doing in there alone all this time. They were inexperienced in the monastic life and had not yet learned that one does not need to be a monk to practice silence and solitude.

One man who takes regular solitary retreats took his cell phone with him last year. He says his seventeen-year-old son called three times a day the first two days. Finally the boy asked, "Are you okay, Dad? Is there something we need to talk about?" Solitude is frightening for some and simply baffling for others.

Our lives require that we keep up a steady pace of do, doing, doing still. It's not that this is a bad thing. But, we so easily begin to understand ourselves, and others, in the context of what we do rather than who we are.

The cloister, or solitude, is as much a state of mind as it is a place. This state of mind develops through the practice of solitude. With an inner solitude in place, you do not mind being alone, because you know you are never alone. You do not resist and fear others, because you know they are not a threat, they can't control you. They do not determine your worth as a human being. You have nothing you must prove to them.

Solitude, rather than driving us into ourselves and away from others, propels us outward and opens us up. It is from the hours spent alone that a monk comes to cherish relationships. It is from the silence that he learns to listen. It is in the deep, empty place inside self that the monk finds God.

We cannot practice genuine Benedictine hospitality unless we have come to it through solitude. We can go through the motions, but the inner opening up does not happen until we have spent a good deal of time alone and a genuine self-love is born. Solitude is built into the monastic life. If you are not a monk, you will have to find ways to build it into yours.

Look for solitude in the snatches of time that hurry past unnoticed. While you wait for a friend to arrive, while the kids are playing, while your spouse watches television, before the household is awake, or after everyone is in bed. Find a quiet place to sit still. Shut the door. Turn off the lights, if this will help, and light a candle.

One woman has a place of solitude on a rickety sunporch attached to the back of her house. It is separated from the house by glass sliding doors. On that porch are a big chair, bookshelves, a crucifix, and a few personal items. If the sliders are pulled and the drapes closed, her family knows it means: "Don't bother me now, please. I need to be alone." On the other hand, when the door is open, others are welcome to join her in that special place.

Somehow, her family understands that they have to mean business if they join her. This is not the place for discussing the weather or the grocery list. That sunporch has become a place where her teenagers talk about their dark secrets and wild dreams, and her husband talked his way through a vocational crisis. Solitude creates a place that is wide enough to make room for others.

Teen retreats at the monastery are a weekend long. At one point in the weekend, the teens are instructed to find a quiet place, alone, and they are given a reflective exercise to complete. It is not a very long exercise and the child is really not alone; lots of other people are in the building. Yet, the young people report that they have never had an experience of solitude before. The usual thing they do if they find themselves alone (and adults do this as well) is to seek company in music or television. The noise companions them, and then they are never really alone with the big *alone* that lives in all of us.

The important thing we learn from these three threads of monasticism is that we must find a way to weave together all the fragments, splinters, and scatterings. Contradictions will always pull at us. We will want time to ourselves while acknowledging the rights others have to our time and energy.

Working through the seeming contradictions that pull us in various directions is always complex. Rather than looking for easy answers, we can model our relationships after the monks and embrace a wide spectrum of relationships, from acceptance of the self to acceptance of the stranger.

The longer we wander through this world the more sure we become that our companions are of utmost importance, as important as our solitude. We don't need to pick solitude over family, or family over other relationships. We need to attentively set our hearts on balancing it all.

Companions give us the support we need to go on. They provide the tenderness of friendship and are a source of stability, wisdom, and growth. We need other people. Some of our companions we choose, such as friends or a spouse. But we are born with a whole set of relationships, for better or worse.

We all are given a family as part of the cost of our humanity. If, by some set of circumstances, we do not have a family, we tend to create one for ourselves. Do we believe these relationships are pure chance? The monks can help us understand that what seems to be chance is God waiting to be discovered. The monk is taught to look for God's presence in every other monk he lives with. He does this with the guys he doesn't particularly like, maybe even more so with the ones he does. He believes that it is no accident that they are together in the monastery.

Our families seem to be rather happenstance. We don't get to pick them, and they almost always come with a lot of weirdness that leaves us toting around a heavy weight for most of our lives. There are few challenges greater than the attempt to be hospitable to those closest to us. Some of it is that they are so close. Some of it is that we assume they will love us, regardless of how we treat them. Some of it, maybe, is just bad habit.

If you asked Father Michael Green, one of the monks and the current Prior of St. Benedict Monastery, for an image of what a monastery is about, he would most likely tell you that it is a family. This is an interesting analogy because the monks are a rare sort of family. They did not grow up together. They don't share a history of celebrations, tragedies, and tradition. The members of the family don't all have the same odd-shaped front teeth and they don't share a last name. They are strangers. They are brothers.

This is very different, in one sense, from our biological families. We do have shared histories, shared jokes, and family legends. We all remember Dad's funeral and we remember the day someone walked out the door and never came back. We are haunted by what someone said twenty-five years ago. But, we are also strangers. It didn't happen overnight. One day you woke up forty years old and realized your sibling is no better known to you than the person next door.

The woman who was mother to a five-year-old is not the same woman who is your mother when you are forty-five. Mothers and fathers give themselves over to caring for their young; they protect and train and shelter. They almost cease to be an individual "me" while they are raising children, and so it is not odd that a child hardly ever knows what their parents' dreams are and have been. They do not know the parent as a real person. They do not know what their father gave up to be their father, and they don't know what their mother's beautiful, deep dream is about.

The day you hear that your father danced on roller skates and your mother sang in nightclubs you experience disorientation, as if it has to be someone else's father or mother being described. Most often we have lines in our skin long before we ever begin to trace the lines of our beloved parent's face, looking for the mystery of who lurks there behind those familiar eyes. About the time we are mature enough to realize our parents are strangers, through no fault of their own, they are taken from us.

We need hospitality in these closest of relationships. Every now and then you get so tired that you just want to be with people who don't require an explanation. Family can be that. People who know why you're tired and have been wishing for a long while that you would put up your feet and shut your eyes.

Even if you do not spend a lot of time with your brothers and sisters, you know, on a gut level, that they understand how you are made, they know from whence you came. You have lived your lives side by side for a lifetime. No, they have not been part of your everyday life, but neither are they oblivious to you. They know where it hurts. They know the long strings of mistakes and second chances you've accumulated. They know the bits and pieces of what, all strung together, makes you who you are today.

The other day I had a spat with my sister, Lorri. We are the only girls in a family of seven siblings.

When I was a little girl with four brothers I prayed for a sister, and I got a beautiful little blonde sister with big blue eyes who stole my heart immediately. We're grownups now and we sometimes disagree. But, every now and then we discover some odd thing we share, which we don't have in common with anyone else in the family, or in the world for that matter.

I have moments when I hear Lorri laugh, or talk, or I see her hands moving, and I'm aware how like each other we really are. We both sleep hugging a pillow, and if you ask either of us what our favorite movie of all time is we will reply *The King and I*. We are both big Don Henley fans. What are the chances unless you are sisters?

But on this particular day we were fighting. We misunderstood each other and pushed each other's buttons. After some pretty intense e-mail bickering, the true Benedictine spirit rose up in me, and I told my little sister to go to hell. To which Lorri replied, "You don't have to care what I think and you probably don't. But I'm not one of your friends you can dismiss, and I'm not going away just because you want me to. I am your sister."

It's hard to get rid of a sister, or a brother, even if you try. And, if by some awful circumstance you do get rid of one for good, it will break your heart forever.

That is what your sister (or brother) gives you—a stubborn, everlasting kind of relationship that will make you weep and make you lose your temper. She knows where you came from. Deny it, suppress it, paint it a different color, and there she is holding on to the truth you would rather not look at today, thank you.

Now all of that is very good for us on one hand. We need to stand in the middle of our messiness and know we are loved and accepted. When a family can offer such acceptance, it is a splendid and holy thing. However, we hit a serious snag in our family relationships when we refuse to let family members grow up, change, and become people who are different from our ideas about them. Yes, we share a history with our family, but there are large sections of history we do not share. Some regions of ourselves are completely unknown to our families. Life changes us from the kids who made sandcastles together so long ago.

In many ways we are exactly like those monks who are strangers and yet family. We are not united by a vow to share life together, but in our families we end up sharing life anyway. We stick in our families because we believe family is important. We do what we consider the right thing, and that's a lot like a vow, so you keep to it in the good and the bad. None of us ever keep our vows perfectly, but vows are still worth making and working very hard to keep—especially when it isn't easy.

By being hospitable with one another, monks give each other permission to be odd or cranky, or just a little off sometimes. There is room in this "family" for those on the edge and those who put you on edge. There is room for the quiet and boisterous, room for the weak and the strong in this family.

Benedict tells his monks to "anticipate one another in honor; most patiently endure one another's infirmities, whether of body or of character" (*The Rule of St. Benedict* 72). God, after all, receives both the glory and the wreck we make of our lives. We owe it to one another to do no less, even in our families. Family is a good place to start practicing hospitality.

However, we must not expect our closest relationships to give us what we can receive only in solitude. We must not expect solitude to give us what only intimate relationships are capable of giving us, and we must not expect that every relationship can bear the full weight of intimacy.

We started out talking about the three strands of monasticism: cloister, community, and hospitality. Each is important. You must spend time alone. It need not be long blocks of time, and you do not have to go far away, but you need a door you can close as well as a place inside of you where you can be in solitude.

We also need others, including people who are not close to our heart of hearts. We need simpler, uncomplicated relationships with others. Hospitality expects that we share ourselves, some part of ourselves at least—some sliver of time, some mere insight, or just a slice of peanut butter pie with someone who needs a slice of peanut butter pie and a smile.

"Benedictine spirituality is intent on the distribution of self for the sake of the other," writes Benedictine author Joan Chittister in *Wisdom Distilled from the Daily*.

In the fall of 1999 a rather odd man appeared in Hazelton, Pennsylvania. He wore a white robe and no shoes. He had long hair and a beard. Residents claim the gloom in that coal mine–wrecked town lifted the day he walked in, and local religious leaders say people showed up in the pews who had abandoned the halls of faith long ago. Carl Joseph—he used to call himself "What'sYourName"—now he goes by James.

He looks like a storybook picture of Jesus right down to the twinkle in his eye. Carl Joseph is about fifty years old; he was raised in Detroit. In the last two decades he has wandered through fourteen countries and forty-seven states (excluding Hawaii, Alaska, and Montana). He's sometimes called the Jesus Guy, but no, he doesn't think he's Jesus. He sees himself as a preacher, nothing more. He says people have been generous and kind, but there was the guy who tossed a soda bottle at him, hitting him in the chest. He finds it amazing that the religious are often the harshest with him. I don't find that amazing or surprising.

While in Pennsylvania, Mr. Joseph received a lot of press, something he did not go looking for; he is much harder to locate now that he is avoiding press coverage. Every now and then a story will surface from a town he has visited. He owns only what he wears, and he lives with whoever opens a door to him. He has been arrested in Ohio twice, for refusing to break up a crowd of teenagers gathered around him.

As many as two thousand people have shown up at one of his town meetings where he talks about love and grace. Then he moves on to the next town, and in his wake, people report that their lives are changed.

It's not hard to figure out that people respond to him the way they do because he is a living icon. They know he isn't Jesus, well of course they know. They aren't stupid folks in Ohio or Pennsylvania. But we *want* Jesus to be among us. We want him to listen; we want him to touch us; we want to hear him laugh and tell us a story.

If Carl Joseph is willing to be an icon, a lot of people are willing to let him. We want God in skin. I heard about a child who was feeling ill. His mother was at work and he was home with a babysitter. The mother called home to tell the sick boy that she loved him and that she is always with him, even when they are apart. The child responded, "But, Mommy, I want someone in skin." That's what we need, you and me and all those hard-to-get others. We just want someone in skin.

Before Father Dan's mother died a few years ago, she became very ill and had to be moved into a nursing facility. It was a bright, clean place with caring, well-trained people. The kind of place where you believe your mother will be safe and cared for carefully. But his mother described the facility best when she said to him, "They kiss you goodnight here." It is human touch that makes us feel most human.

We become more available as the one "in skin" for others as we move toward a healthy balance in our relationships. Balance gives us freedom, eases anxieties, and makes room in our lives. Cloister, community, and hospitality—they represent this balance. Enter each deeply. Know the depths of solitude, enjoy the warmth of community, and take a hand in the companionship of hospitality. By gently and gradually gathering up the strands of your fragmented life into one whole, you will become the one in skin that can distribute yourself to others and still have something left to take into the great solitude of your vast soul to rest in God.

six

Preparing a Table

Uncle Stan dies in Cleveland and you find yourself sitting at a table with cousins you haven't seen in years and great uncles you did not even remember. The death is a sad thing, but there at the tables during lunch you hear stories about your dad. You hear how your parents met. Someone remembers the time you visited cousin Linda and cried to go home to your mother, but Linda is gracious enough not to mention you were a big, strong boy of eleven at the time.

The table is a place where you connect and belong. It is a place where the past remains alive in the memory of the very old, and the future sparkles with possibility. It is enchanted. We lean close together, we share a glass, we tell a story. Through this simple human relating, the universe feels as though it is right again, even after Uncle Stan has gone on to whatever comes next.

We all have memories of tables prepared for us and those we have readied for others. Some of the memories are from childhood. Others are memories of good friends, of falling in love, or of deeply connecting with another human being. Meals are powerful symbols in our memory. But someone has to make a meal happen.

Someone must consider it important enough to give themselves to the work that goes into preparation. Setting a table and making ready for a meal involves preliminary thought and consideration for others. To do it right you have to think through your guest's preferences and history; you need to know if they have allergies or chronic illnesses. If you invite more than one guest, you must consider which of them would enjoy sitting together and how they might relate. Preparing for another pulls us out of ourselves—that is one of the good gifts of hospitality.

The image of preparing a table, or preparing a place, is a good overall image for hospitality. In genuine hospitality we work to make our entire existence a welcoming table, a place prepared for others to be at ease, to receive from us comfort and strength. Hospitality teaches me to work at becoming someone who is easy to be with, as either guest or host.

Hospitality becomes a way of life as we become more open. It will not happen without preparation and unless you intend it to happen. When we speak of "preparing a table," we refer to the intention and the work of making space for another human being. Preparing a table has sacramental meaning for Benedictines. Every meal, like every encounter with a human being, has the potential to reveal God present in Creation. The table represents the unknown yearning of every human heart for communion with the "something more" that infuses all that exists.

A lifetime of ignoring the sounds of the soul has deafened us to this universal desire, but some little part of us can't forget and waits eagerly for the moment bread is broken, a hand is given, a laugh fills the air, and then by chance or grace, a connection to someone happens that magically opens us up in places we didn't know existed.

Food is basic to human existence, but it is more than it seems to be; it represents the More. In the Christian tradition, bread and wine are sacramental, carrying to us the presence of God. The use of a table, utensils, bread, and wine as the means by which Christians receive God is a family symbol. We receive Christ through simple foods, simple utensils, from a guy in a dress (at least in the more liturgical forms of Christianity) who cleans up and puts away the dishes when he's done.

In every family meal, in every dinner between friends, in every meal where monks go to table, a sacramental mystery is present. There is magic in these connections that does something to us way down deep. The lesson is that we must take seriously our receiving of others. Whether we are cooking a meal, mowing the grass, scouring the sinks, or painting a wall, we are preparing for the Sacred to come to us.

The monastery feeds dozens of teenagers almost every weekend during the school year. Brother Antony is the one who sets the tables. Besides being a monk, Antony is an artist. If you watch him setting tables in the retreat house you will probably guess he is an artist, even if you have never seen his studio. He prepares the tables for the teens with a sense of reverence that is obvious and humbling. He is setting places for pizza and soda, but he does so with the same care he uses when he prepares the table for Eucharist.

Antony understands that in preparing a table, he is not just setting a place to eat. He is making room for one of God's children. He is creating a space for a human being, and human beings are sacred. This means you do it right, you pay attention, you get out of yourself and whatever else might be occupying your mind.

The quieter teens especially respond to Antony, maybe because he's quiet himself. He moves behind the scenes of the retreat, preparing and putting people at ease, weaving his wondrous magic of beauty in everything he touches.

Many young adults who go to the monastery will remember that retreat weekend for all their life. Many of them return to the monks to baptize their children and solemnize their marriages. They visit for Easter and Christmas. They show up when the bottom has fallen out of their lives. Most of them leave the monastery knowing someone cares.

Father Dan says that is because the monks take care in the little things—like Brother Antony setting the table as if he were creating a work of art. Antony is Benedictine and he has heard over and over that the tools of the monastery are sacred. He understands that places and things mediate God. There was one incident, Dan remembers, when he really got to see the heart of Brother Antony.

"Because his understanding of Benedictine reverence for all things goes so deep, I should not have been surprised when his protective urges took over on one retreat. It is usual for the retreat team to tell the teens that when the pizza arrives they have to eat in an orderly fashion, not taking more than they can eat, and waiting for grace to be said.

"For some reason the pizza arrived one Sunday without one of us having issued the standard warning, and the kids converged on the pizza man with all the hormonal energy you can imagine in a fifteen-year-old.

"I was in the lower living room when Brother Antony came running down the steps and halted halfway, his face flushed. He said in his regal way, 'Father Dan, come at once. There's a chaos up here!' Then he turned on his heel and ran back to defend the retreat house with his last breath. You have to admire a guy who takes on forty-five hungry kids for the sake of what he considers holy."

The deep meaning of hospitality involves our entrance into the mess of things; it means we run right into the chaos if that's what it takes. If we do this, there is a slow, mysterious something that happens, transforming the riot into something good. Naturally, the hard thing is stopping ourselves from making for the door when the chaos happens. The hard thing is throwing ourselves headlong into the riot and trusting the reality of transformation.

We aren't going to run toward the riot unless we think transformation is worthwhile. The retreat house at St. Benedict's was designed with teenagers in mind. The monks, architect, and workers kept this goal carefully in sight. It was built to be a shelter for teens, and it was meant to be the kind of shelter they would remember all their lives.

That is the kind of shelter hospitality offers: the staying kind. The purposes of hospitality are not as simple as providing comfort for a night or a week. The best kind of hospitality seeps into your soul and shapes your identity. We can give this kind of hospitality to each other only if we take the time to prepare sheltering places around us and inside of us. The table set for the teens is one example of hospitality. But you set other kinds of tables all your life. We all eat and drink with others; rarely would we elect to dine alone. When you ask someone to your table, as these teens are invited to the monks' table at the retreat house, you include them, you make them part of "us."

There are times when the food we share is a sign of connection and acceptance, times such as weddings, funerals, anniversaries, birthdays, graduations, family reunions, and religious professions. At these events food is a sign of unity and singleness of purpose. In Latin, the word *companion* literally means to "break bread" together. No wonder the Eucharist has such power. It is founded in our food experience, and our earliest experience of that is associated with warmth and touching. Food is powerful. It says, "You belong here."

It isn't just food we pass out that nourishes or impoverishes the human heart. The table, for the teacher or social worker, is her or his desk. Whatever the specific physical structures of your work might be, you give something to others from them. You create a space for others because work is always for the service of others.

In the ancient world (the one Jesus was born into), people saw the sharing of meals as having eternal consequences. If you ate meals with the right kind of people, paradise waited for you. If you ate with the wrong kind of people . . . well, you get it. Jesus challenged this organizing principle of his culture. Understanding how the culture viewed having the "right" dinner companions shines a whole new light on the old story of feeding the five thousand.

In the gospel story of Jesus feeding multitudes, we marvel at a little bit of food feeding a whole bunch of people and miss a whole other point. Jesus wanted them to *EAT* together. If they did this, it would change everything, they would be joining the revolution. Eating together, for them, was transforming.

There's something to think about the next time we're washing windows or trimming the hedge. When we take an open stance toward others in all that we do, the work of our hands takes on transforming power. And that is a little thing we can do every day of our lives. We can pay attention to how we wax the floor and park the car because we are growing in awareness that the work we do is work for others.

Our preparations for others remind us that we are not alone in the world. Not only are we not alone, others are counting on us. Many years ago the monastery had a novice, an older novice who had the responsibility of ringing the bell that called the monks to prayer. He fell asleep early one night and woke up suddenly, thinking it was early. It was actually 10:30 PM. He looked at his watch upside-down and thought he was twenty minutes late ringing the bell.

He rushed outside to the courtyard in his underwear, with his pants wrapped around his neck, and started ringing the bell as if everything in the world depended on what he was doing. Another monk, visiting from a sister monastery in Australia, stuck his head out the window and yelled in his Aussie way, "You bloomin' ass, it's only half past ten!" Nope, not even your best efforts will always be understood and appreciated.

Despite this, the novice recognized that his work was a service to others, a service he took seriously enough to run into the cold night in his underwear. (He told the other monks later that he wrapped the pants around his neck so he wouldn't catch cold.)

You can prepare for others every day in countless ways, and not just in the work you do from 9 to 5. You prepare for others when you plan a quiet time with your child, when you set candles on the dinner table, when you shovel your sidewalk or trim the tree away from the street sign. These are ways of preparing to receive others—in other words, through these activities you prepare a table for others. When we are preparing a table, we are also preparing ourselves.

Our ability to make room for others, and the joy we do or do not find in such activity, depends largely on our experience of being accepted or not. We build shelter for others because somewhere along the way someone sheltered us and thereby taught our hungry hearts how to love. Every little lesson along the way has accumulated to account for how we are able to love today.

Your memories of sheltering places may take you to a retreat house like Subiaco, or perhaps to your childhood. Our preparations create these sheltering places. Every childhood has them. Even children who are neglected or abused find sheltering places. Most of us don't have childhoods with such an extreme need for shelter. Instead, we have memories of rain falling on the roof of the porch, and we remember how safe and dry it felt there. Or, we remember the day the wind straight-lined across the woods and the only cover we could find was under the stairs, where Mom read a book and we sang while the wind roared.

Those are the kinds of shelters that hold you during difficult times, long after the storm has passed. Those are the sorts of shelters that families hope they can be for their children.

Each summer day when she was a toddler, Gina and I napped under the whirling fan of the vaulted ceiling in the master bedroom. She smelled of chlorine from her little pool where she spent the morning under the trees that surround our cabin in the woods. She smelled of peanut butter and sugary soda clinging to fingers wrapped tightly around her once-pink, but now very faded, bunny. She kept a thumb in her mouth. Her caramel brown hair was sun-streaked, and her long limbs were honey tan from the sunshine.

We napped from 1:00 to 2:30 each day on the big bed, and before I fell asleep I would remember sleeping on a sun-porch under the eaves of a house long ago. It was summer then, too, and raining. I don't know if this is actually a memory or a dream I recall. But I felt utterly safe in that place, just as Gina did under the whirling fan in a house sheltered by tall oaks and pines.

There are spaces God creates like the deep quiet woods around our cabin, and there are spaces we make: our homes, offices, and the places we go to for the specific purpose of hearing God.

Where Gina sleeps at the cabin is under the sharp slope of the steep roof. It is a space otherwise useless except for storage. She slept there on two feather beds, three old quilts, and a sundried yellow checkered sheet. Her little pillow has blue and white ticking; she refuses to use a pillowcase. There is a shelf that runs the length of her space. It's filled with odds and ends, much of it meaning nothing to anyone but Gina and me. When she was a little girl we called it her "special place" (which sounded better than saying that she slept in a big closet).

Driftwood and shells from a walk on the beach, rocks collected from the bridge, a doll my daughter, her mother, loved as a little girl, a Madonna figure given to her by our very kind neighbor Florence. A dream-catcher hangs over her head. We got it at a local gift shop the morning after she had a bad dream. We agreed it would block all bad dreams.

I learned from the monastery that physical structures are more than brick, glass, and wood. Not that a building or home needs to be lavish to create a sense of security and shelter. Instead, we need to take care to create spaces where the soul can unfurl its wings and the toddler can wiggle her toes. This kind of care is in the details; it is revealed in our passion to prepare a place for someone. When we really care about someone, we try a bit harder.

The process of creating sheltering places causes us to think about the fears, needs, and vulnerabilities of others. We can't consciously create shelter without acknowledging that sometimes we don't feel safe. And oddly enough, the security we crave can come to us in the smallest of ways: clean sheets, a simple but lovingly prepared meal, a soft light to read by until the dark isn't so dark.

Often, we don't give much thought to the kinds of places we are creating as we shape our homes. But what we make is holy. The work of human hands—monasticism has always considered that a sacred thing. We don't always notice it; sometimes this elusive reality strikes us at the oddest times.

The other day I accompanied my granddaughter Chelsea to a local carnival during one of the many small-town festivals scattered all over Michigan in late summer. From early June to late August, this had been the summer when Chelsea overcame a certain set of fears. She had ridden the big rides at the amusement park, including a rollercoaster. She had hooked up to the wire and shot down the zip line at camp. We were at the carnival so she could ride the Tornado over and over and over for her eleventh birthday. She had looked her giant in the eye. She had overcome fear and we were there to celebrate.

I can't explain what happened. I was standing in the parking-lot-turned-carnival during the fleeting days of a warm Michigan summer. The Tornado was lemon bright, its cars painted gold and sparkly as it roared my Chelsea up and around, as she spun and sang and waved her arms gleefully—alone on the ride. The young conqueror of dragons was on a victory ride. Classic rock blasted from speakers, seagulls flew overhead, and we were assaulted with the fatty, sugary smells of elephant ears nearby. Chelsea wore rose-colored glasses, dangly earrings, and a bright T-shirt with a flower in her dark hair. Young and brave, she had overcome, and there in the mix with the whirling and the beating of the music, I could not look at the determined, courageous child without tears.

Right there, at a carnival, in the crazy mix of human contraptions, noise, and the warm breezes of summer, serendipity caught up with us. It was carried on the breezes of summer and the twirling of a carnival ride and the throbbing, husky sounds of Bob Seger. The work of God, the work of human hands came together to construct a split second of rare lucidity and joy—a reality that had not existed only seconds before.

At St. Benedict Monastery the monks have built a chapel that, regardless of how often you go there, has the power to steal your breath, startle your eyes, and move your soul. The chapel appears to have been raised up from the dust of the earth in a primal whirl of wind. It is a lot of glass and wood and modern architecture at its best, an architectural wonder, actually. But it is much more than excellent architecture.

What the chapel has in common with the carnival in a resort town in Michigan is that it is the work of human hands; it was conceived in a human mind and crafted by human beings who were preparing a place for other human beings. This was always the intention of the monks as they planned the chapel. They wanted it to be a place where the weary could get away and pray, a place where a little bit of peace had a chance of getting hold of you.

The chapel is the place where the monks go to pray day after day, several times each day. It is at the heart of their community. It is also the place where they share their prayer and their life with the stranger at the door. It is where their friends and oblates gather, worship, learn, pray, think.

Preparing a place is something that all of us can do. In human labor an astonishing thing happens: God shows up. As we make ready a place for others, something happens inside of us: we are prepared also. The Benedictine motto is "Pray and work." Benedictines consider work holy. Human labor is a reflection of divine work. Human labor is shared with God. Work expresses our humanity, and it gives us a chance to use our gifts. This mystical element to work expresses a sacramental understanding of life. Work requires reverence and it teaches us of our value.

Former Eagles drummer Don Henley was very Benedictine when he wrote these lines in one of his songs, "Whatever your hands find to do, you must do with all your heart."

Through the many months the monks spent building their gloriously simple chapel, the community was preparing itself as well. They were making a conscious choice to include nonmonastics as part of their daily lives. The chapel allowed easier access to the monks. Before they had the new chapel, a visitor had to walk through the monastery to reach the chapel. People tended to be a little cautious about doing that, but the new chapel meant that people could join them for prayer or mass anytime. They could go and sit in the silence. People would be coming and going more than ever before.

The internal community preparations were subtle. Even the most introverted of monks began spending a few minutes with people after mass on Sunday. While the chapel was being raised up, relationships also were built. The monks were being true to their vision of opening up to God's people and welcoming them to share the journey.

At the same time, the monks had to prepare to guard their way of life, to set up boundaries that would protect the monastic community. Benedict made it clear to his monks that yes, they must open to strangers and welcome the stranger as if God were walking through the door. Benedict also told his monks, however, that after a greeting and a prayer they should excuse themselves from the guest. The monk had to learn to honor boundaries for himself and for the guest.

As they prepared for a new phase in their monastic life, the monks consciously made choices that would be welcoming. They paid attention to the details, such as providing a nursery for young children, determining how many people could be comfortable in the space, considering where the sun might hit the eyes of the people in the choir stalls and chairs. They worked on making sure that people would be able to hear no matter where they were seated in the chapel. They included meeting space for small groups and a place to prepare a cup of coffee.

They included plans for a gift shop where, for the first time, guests would be able to buy a candle made by Brother Jim, or a painting from the heart of Brother Antony, or notecards designed by the printer monk, Father Mike. They offered not only space, but also their gifts and talents.

The monks have a life together, but they have chosen to care for others on a daily basis just as they care for themselves. To do so is to be human. As we wash our bodies and fold our clothing and shovel the driveway, we indicate that we have accepted our role and life, as it exists. We are making peace with ourselves and all the others around us.

When we fail to brush our teeth, wash our feet, and get enough sleep, we are heading for detachment from the real self and from others; we are folding in on ourselves. A person who is disconnecting from life will usually have symptoms of depression and addictive behaviors. It is also common for them to stop taking care of themselves in the everyday small details like clean socks.

Attention to the details is a way to prepare a place for others. There is no one who does this better at St. Benedict Monastery than Father John Martin. Through the years I've come to appreciate John Martin for his ability to keep ducks in a row and all things on schedule. He is careful when he prepares for liturgies. This attention to detail made him especially well-suited to coordinate the monastery's oblate program. When he is given any task, he takes every detail very seriously. And if you should be fortunate enough to go on vacation with him, he will also prepare thoroughly for that.

At John Martin's solemn profession, I met a friend of his who had once taken a vacation with John

Martin. He told me how John Martin had every day planned and would pull out his list whenever they tried to figure out what came next. He did not object to spontaneity, but if he had a plan and it was a good plan, you stuck to it. After all, John Martin had laid out the plan for your vacation enjoyment. He had prepared a place for you—enjoy.

Preparing a place says "welcome" and "you are accepted and honored." Few can resist such a welcome. In all our preparations for the other who comes to us, we will end up a little surprised. As we do the work of preparation, we prepare ourselves too and, something more, we are prepared by the divine presence. The work of preparation opens us up. We begin consciously to turn our will toward receiving others.

The work can be as simple as washing sheets for the guest room, baking a cake for the family who just lost their grandmother, or gathering wildflowers to put on the family table. You can paint a room at the homeless shelter. You can teach someone how to change the oil in her car.

Set an extra place at your table tonight and receive God who comes among us. Light a candle and take a deep breath and receive the presence of the One who is always with you. Remember this: there is a place prepared for you. It is a place where you can rest. It is a place where you are renewed and changed.

The work you do that prepares a home or a building or a yard to welcome others is very important work. It is holy work. But it is not the most important work of preparation. The most important work is preparing yourself to receive others. Only you know what you need to do to make that happen. Is there someone to forgive? Is there someone to release? Is there a fear to abandon? Is there an attitude to adjust? We all have weapons to lay down and battles to call off before we can open up our hearts.

Ultimately, hospitality is not about the table you set, or the driveway you plow. Hospitality is about preparing the holiest of holies. It is about the heart you make ready. Yours.

seven

Companionship and Intimacy

*I*f we are going to love others, we need to understand that the nature of love is not static, fixed, and predictable. There are zillions of degrees of intimacy in relationships. Even within a single relationship, the degree of intimacy will vary from week to week and year to year. This is important to remember, if we are going to avoid our feelings being trampled on constantly and our expectations frustrated.

Hospitality ultimately involves us with others, and we will become tangled up in relationships. We need to be aware that each of these relationships will be different from the next and will vary in degrees of closeness. But intimacy is the goal of hospitality, and in order to understand that, we need to look at the meaning of *intimacy* and *companionship*. We no longer have clear definitions of these words.

Having said there are degrees of intimacy, let's focus on two kinds of relating: intimacy and companionship. All of us get confused about how much we should reveal in a relationship, how much we should give, and how much we should let someone give us. Confusion is inevitable since we are daily bludgeoned with messages that tell us emotionally, spiritually healthy people *always* connect to others in a profound way.

Are we cold and heartless because we do not want to be intimate with every single person who crosses our paths? No. It isn't possible to achieve such a thing. We will have some very close relationships and we will have companionable ones. The media gives us the wrong idea about less intense relationships. They tell us that any relationship that is not intimate is unimportant, and so we have dismissed less-than-intimate relationships.

This is dangerous. We need relationships of depth, but we also need companionable relationships in which we listen to the other, show that we care, and are present to another person, even when tired or cranky. This kind of companionship is a healing thing for both the giver and the receiver, but it is not easy. It means we put our own feelings aside. Sounds easy until we have to do it.

Every relationship does *not* have to involve gut-level sharing. It is a beautiful thing to simply respond to others' everyday, simple needs. Reassure someone that they are stronger than they know. Include the shy person in the conversation. Notice the well-executed report or talk. Offer a cup of tea to someone who looks tired.

Maybe someone just needs to be left alone. Listen when people talk. It is impossible to exaggerate the number of people who never feel heard, even by friends, family, or spouse. Being a person of hospitality involves getting out of self for long enough periods that you can hear other people—really hear them—and pay attention to what they might need at this moment.

Some people are very good at this; it seems to come naturally. The rest of us have to work at it. Father Dan has often said that Brother Benedict, the oldest of the monks in his community, has been his companion for forty years and that he has felt this companionship deeply.

Yet they have never sat down and had what we would call a "heart-to-heart." Brother Benedict is profoundly present to people without even trying. If you asked him how he has managed such a thing, he would not even know what you are talking about. His life of prayer has poured a hospitable spirit into him.

"He is a constant presence to me," Father Dan says. "Even though we have talked about deep and serious things, we haven't told each other our stories. But he is sensitive to what I feel; I have tried to emulate this in him."

Emulating someone is a good way to learn hospitality. Find a hospitable person and spend time with them. Listen to them. Do not look for methods or tips from them. Just be together and you will be astonished at what happens.

In Benedict's entire adulthood, this holy old man has probably never had what anyone else would consider an intimate relationship. He is kind and good to all, and people love him. Recently he was in the hospital. Father Dan said he couldn't help noticing how all the nurses fell in love with the old monk. When he visited, they would tell him what a kind and sweet man Brother Ben is; they fell over each other to take care of him.

"I know Brother Benedict and he did nothing out of the ordinary," Dan said. "He was just himself, sometimes sweet, sometimes grumpy, sometimes bewildered, but always real. I took him home from the hospital and told him some of the very nice things the nurses had said about him. He waved it off and said, 'Oh, they say that about everyone.'"

Brother Ben is an excellent companion, not just to the monks, but to anyone God places in his life that day. He is almost completely deaf. This makes it hard for him to get to know the people who come to the monastery for mass on Sunday or during the week. Yet, when he was sick, there was an outpouring of concern for him because people cared about him. They had felt his love for all of them without ever having a single intimate moment with him.

Since he's recovered, he has become the most popular monk with the Sunday crowd. During the passing of the peace people jam to be with him. He sits in the very front of the chapel, and he just turns and touches hands and smiles and makes a sign of peace at people. Father Dan says he thinks of it as his Jay Leno imitation. They all want a piece of him and he gives the best he can.

Through the years, Father Dan has observed instances when he can tell, at a gut level, that Brother Ben cares deeply. It is unmistakable. He reveals his caring in a comment, or a pat on the back, or a joke. His deep, companionable nature has been easier for Dan to receive and cherish than the efforts other monks have made at intimacy before a relationship has grown to the point that intimacy happens naturally.

Whether you have been married or not, you may have noticed that marriage and even close friendships are similar to Brother Ben's way of companionship. Marriage has moments of intimacy, but for the most part operates on a companionable level day to day. There are kids to bathe, dogs to clip, and groceries to fetch. Someone has to rake the leaves and someone has to get the cat off the roof. There is no time for intimate discussions while little Tommy is finger-painting on the guestroom walls.

There was a morning drive-time show in Flint, Michigan, that asked callers to talk about what made a marriage work. As you'd expect, they received many calls about communication and romance and telling the other person what you enjoy sexually. Each of these callers thought they had the one answer to the big question. Someone suggested a date night. Someone suggested a fantasy night. All fine ideas—if you can pull it off. Most married people can't; life just doesn't happen that way.

It was one of the disc jockeys that, in the end, said the most sensible and reassuring thing of all. He said, "You have to be able to look across the room, after the kid has trashed it, and you're scrubbing the rug while your mate is wiping grape jelly off the kid's face and think, Dear God, I am so happy. I can sit with her and do nothing. I can dance with her on the deck under the stars in our backyard. I can tell her my wildest dream and she won't laugh out loud. She doesn't even care that I watch football. This is great, even though it isn't what I expected. It's better than that."

Companionship is the great gift in marriage. Intimacy does not happen from the first cup of coffee until the light goes off at night. Such a thing would just be too much. Too often, we have too many unrealistic expectations of marriage, and they spill over into our other relationships.

Doing life together, as monks and married couples do, provides an anchor of stability. Most relationships today are less stable than they were fifty years ago. Families are no longer held together by economic security, religious tradition, and cultural expectations, and the extended family has a lesser role in the lives of most couples. Most people experience the shattering of family ties, if not personally, then within their closest sphere of family and friends.

Just as a monastic community creates a shelter for others, a couple creates a life-giving shelter when their union is a healthy and loving one. Love, by its nature, is life-giving. This does not mean that all couples become parents; producing children is not essential to loving each other. A couple creates a family, and if not biologically, then they do so in other ways. When a couple doesn't love well enough to open their borders and, out of the strength of their love, welcome others, the union will collapse on itself and become destructive. The same is true in the monastery.

No matter how intimate a relationship, that single relationship is not enough to satisfy the human hunger for love. No human being has enough love to meet such needs. Only our passion for God is enough love; only God's passion for us can make us whole. Most of us will have intimate relationships, but we make a mistake if we think that intimacy is all we need. We also need companions, we need good fun, we need the brief and tender moment when a stranger stoops to help collect the clutter that has dropped to the floor. Moments like these help us remember that the universe is a safe and welcoming place. We come fully awake.

Marriage and intimate relationships are safe places where you can relax and let down the pretenses. We all need such places. Benedict tells his monks to make the monastery such a place. Even the daily reality of intimate relationships may not feel intimate a lot of the time. But the support and strength of intimacy will be there when you need it if the relationship is solid and both people are capable of intimate bonding.

Intimacy does not consist of a constant level of relating; instead, it simply happens when it needs to, if people are open and able to enter the moment. Many years ago, while Father Dan was serving the Detroit parish, he received a call that one of the parish families had just had a terrible tragedy. Their eldest son had taken his own life.

In the days following the young man's death, Father Dan visited their home. He had not been close to the family. He knew them, but they were not friends. He watched as the mother became inconsolable and the father lost himself in a drunken stupor.

He could not imagine the pain this couple was feeling. He did not judge the couple for how they were handling their son's death. None of us know what we would do if such a thing happened. They had no room inside them for anything but the pain. The boy was not the only child in the family, however; they also had a little girl, five or six years old.

Dan remembers, "I went over to check on the family and found the mother locked in her bedroom and the father sitting in a chair, completely intoxicated and basically unconscious. The little girl was sitting on the floor sobbing, with her frail little shoulders heaving and her eyes red from so much crying that you wondered if her little body could handle the force of all the pain. She was completely alone in her grief, not because her parents were cruel or uncaring, but because they were shattered.

"I picked up the child, and without saying a word, put her on my lap and sat in a rocking chair. I held her and rocked while she cried for a couple of hours. A bond formed between us instantly."

Dan did not become a friend of the family. Once they had come through the crisis he was again just a parish priest. Yet he shared with that little girl one of the most profoundly intimate connections he can ever remember. He lost all thought of himself. There was an understanding between them that was beyond words. Mutual reverence and not warm, fuzzy social comforts is the climate of Benedictine hospitality.

We have lost completely the awareness that relationships come in degrees. We don't know how to move from casual to intimate and back again. We have forgotten that we ought to pour ourselves out sometimes, and hold back at other times.

Discretion requires you to respect someone without trying to be their best friend. Hospitality is not a call to unquestioning intimacy with the whole world. Monks are not flower children, and the monastery meal is not a love-in. Hospitality is a call to revere what is sacred in every person ever born. While intimacy does not have to happen in every instance of hospitality, reverence does. We reverence people not because they are pleasant, but because God is present in them.

Intimacy is what we crave; it is also what we fear most. A major problem with any discussion about intimacy is that the word itself is confusing and the meaning of it is relative. Intimacy happens in companionable relationships, and companionship happens in intimate relationships.

Equating sex with intimacy contributes to our misunderstanding the true nature of intimacy. If a couple has had sex we call it being intimate. When people discuss their dating relationships, sometimes they ask, "Have you been intimate?" They mean, have you had sex yet? We call women's lingerie "intimate apparel." It is no wonder that we do not know the meaning of intimacy. Nearly all popular culture references to intimacy are wrapped up in sexual connotation.

In reporting an acquaintance rape situation one news reporter stated, "He had been intimate with her for six months." Sex does not automatically create intimacy, as millions of people have painfully discovered. In making sex and intimacy one and the same, intimacy has been belittled, while an entire set of faulty expectations of casual sex has been created.

When we confuse intimacy with sexual relations, we imply that sex is the only means to closeness and that sex generates intimacy. The truth is that sex strengthens a bond between two people who love and nurture one another, but it is also the tool of much cruelty and abuse. Sex does not equal intimacy.

To imply that our deepest needs are met only by sexual encounters has set up an entire generation to be disillusioned. Sex can happen between two people who don't even like each other. It can be used as a weapon and as a reward system. People can be demeaned by sex. Sex can be beautiful and make you a better person, or it can crush you. Intimacy, however, never crushes the human soul; it only builds it up. Because intimacy regards the other as valuable and cherished, it makes us more human.

Dozens of relationships involve intimacy, including parental and family ones. To make intimacy explicitly sexual is to suggest that these closest relationships are less than intimate. When I experience genuine intimacy, I know to the bone that I am not alone. This knowing comes through relationship. It is not a thing I realize with my brain, but a thing I discover with my heart. Intimacy feels familiar, yet sometimes the deep sustaining power of intimacy jolts your sleepy heart wide awake and everything becomes brighter and better.

Intimacy is the deep experience of knowing another human heart. The right kind of sex is certainly intimate, but we must not forget that sex happens without intimacy all the time. By confusing sex and intimacy, we use sex in the hope of experiencing intimacy. To be intimate is to be figuratively naked, without walls, completely open to another human being. That sort of intimacy makes for wonderful sex.

In our culture the attraction of sex is excitement and pleasure, but most people are craving to be known when they have sex, even if they don't understand the primal drives that compel them toward others in sexual union.

Without intimacy, sex only deepens abiding and severe loneliness. The purpose of sex is to enhance an already intimate relationship; when we use it for any other purpose it fails us. Our bodies are linked to who we are, after all; we cannot exist in this life without a body. What you do to my body you do to me. This makes casual sex devastating. Sex means something; it says something. Casual sex lies. Faithless sex, based on nothing but the urge to mate, is a violation of my person—it is definitely not intimacy.

Lyrics to a recent rock song proclaim, "When everything's made to be broken, I just want you to know who I am." This is a cry for intimacy. Another song says, "I don't know if I've ever been touched by a hand that loves me." When a gifted songwriter lets you into his or her inner regions, you hear in their music the human heart crying for intimacy rather than sex. It's a common theme in the arts, a reflection of the human soul.

Intimacy has also come to mean "personal." We see a couple of close friends talking and think, "I won't interrupt an intimate moment." We think of secrets as intimate, and associate them with the private and personal. In using the language in this way, we further muddy the meaning of intimacy and relegate intimacy to the most private realms of human experience. We don't make room for intimacy in companionable kinds of relationships or in the everyday events of our lives, in the way we welcome others and open our hearts to them.

Intimacy is the experience of sharing life together. When Father Dan talks about his relationship with Brother Ben he is speaking out of a lifetime shared. But intimacy happens in other ways every day and it happens in extraordinary circumstances as well.

Intimacy happened in America when every American we knew was sitting in front of a television watching the events of September 11, 2001, unfold. We suddenly felt connected to a bigger whole that consists of all of us from sea to shining sea. We experienced a brief period of knowing we are part of one another and we belong to each other. That was an experience of intimacy we shared with strangers, the people next door, and our best friends.

You may remember the CEO of a big financial firm that had been housed in the World Trade Center sobbing on television, struggling to make comprehensible words, and finally describing his reaction to the horror by saying, "I went home and kissed my children."

That same night I was at our family cabin in the woods. Along with millions of Americans, at 7:00 PM, I lit a candle and I tried to pray. Taking the candle out to the front porch, I sat quietly and listened to the sounds of the woods in a place so far removed and different from the ashes in New York City. With all the miles between us, I was much like the Wall Street guy on television; my soul could only weep. We were together in that, all of us hardly able to do anything but sob.

We gathered to watch the memorial service from the National Cathedral and listened to Billy Graham say in a faltering voice, "I am an old man now. The older I get, the more I cling to hope." And we all clung to hope together.

We watched when the lights on Broadway came back on. Matthew Broderick said, "It's dark right now, but tonight the lights are on again." The same night Nathan Lane said, "You can't dim the joy in this country." Joy isn't a word you hear people use very often. The actor was on to something. Genuine joy doesn't usually happen until you've been to the depths of despair. It is not like happiness. Joy is the internal passion that remains after the evil's best attempts to knock the life out of you. If America has ever had a chance to realize real joy, this is it.

You might remember the volunteer firefighters. One who had gone to New York within days of the attack talked about what it was like for him to be at Ground Zero. He was a big man with a ponytail and a red kerchief tied around his head. He looked like his nose had been broken a couple times. He was the kind of guy you cross the street to avoid. There he was, on national television, with tears streaming down his face as he said, "We are all family now. I love everyone."

Next week he might be singing, "Are you ready for some football?" but that day he looked toward heaven and whispered, "We are going to be crying for a long time." We never expected to have a place in America we would call Ground Zero, and if that is not enough to make a tough guy cry, nothing could.

Father Dan was in Rome, on community business, on September 11. He was there with one other American monk, Father Livy, his traveling companion and a brother monk from Detroit. While the two men have belonged to the same congregation and have known each other for decades, they don't have an intimate friendship.

Yet, when the attacks happened, Dan recalled feeling suddenly connected to the only other American there and being glad he was with him. It had been incredibly difficult to be away from America during that period. Dan wanted to go home to be with the monks, his family, his friends; but no one could return until air space was opened up again.

Dan remembers going through customs when he finally returned to the United States. "The customs official looked at my papers and said something about I must have been in Rome on church business. I nodded, and then he looked me in the eye and said, 'Welcome home, Father.' Customs officials had never said that before. I wanted to hug him. Everything had changed."

All these years later, it is easy to be cynical and question the sincerity, or importance, of the connection we all felt to one another in the immediate days and weeks following the New York and Pentagon attacks. For the most part, Americans are back to being Marlboro men and women and pumping up our own importance and independence to an unreasonable extent.

Intimacy will only happen as we set aside our prejudices and fears. Intimacy happens when we least expect it, and it shows up in odd situations between strangers. It makes strangers into brothers and sisters. It flares up and gives us an emotional rush of acceptance and belonging and being known, and then it ebbs away, always there to wash over us when we need a shoulder to lean on, a hand to clutch, or a joke that will make us laugh all the way to our toes.

Among the most unforgettable images that have emerged from the American tragedy is the number of people who called home with their last breath. Whether Muslim, Christian, Jew, or nonbeliever, they called from the fifty-second floor of the World Trade Center or from a hijacked plane with the same message. They used their last breath to say, "I love you. Whatever happens, remember the love." To say, " I love . . ." is an affirmation of life at its highest and holiest. To say, "I love . . ." is to say, "I live, I am human, and you have made me more human. I will always live in you who love me."

My husband, David, and I lost a good friend in the days just before September 11. David had gone to high school with his wife. We had all taken country-and-western dance classes together. We had shared many a pizza, burger, and rib with them. Joe was a lot like Brother Ben.

He was one of those people who could make you feel like the only person in the room when he talked to you. Yet, he wasn't the kind to make an effort at intimacy. He didn't wake up in the morning and say, "Today I am going to bond intimately with other people." He just got out of bed and spent his days making other people feel like they mattered.

He and David were both part of a service club, and whenever the club got off course and more interested in socializing than service, Joe was one of the people who would kick them back on track again. As diabetes stole his sight, he would make jokes about being a blind guy. His disability never kept him from living with a great deal of joy and enthusiasm.

If you had asked Joe about the meaning of intimacy, he would have looked at you with bewilderment. An answer would have failed him. But then he would have poured another cup of coffee, he would have taken you bowling, or told a joke, and you would leave him feeling taller, stronger, and more human.

My husband David, a United Methodist minister, officiated at the funeral for Joe. At the end of it he said, "Go and serve the way Joe served. Go and put joy in the life of others the way Joe did. Go and love the way Joe loved."

This is the message from the people who called from the heights that were about to crash down around all of us and change our world forever: "Go and love in memory of me." This is the message of Benedict to his monks: "Live and love in the name of Jesus."

The ancient monk Benedict must have known that his celibate monks would discover the magic of intimacy not only in each other, but in the stranger at the door. So he told them to keep the door open and greet the stranger as if you are greeting God. Benedict is sane and sensible about the whole thing. He tells his monks to greet the guests and honor the guests and then get back to what you were doing. Hospitality thrives in the monastery because every single day there is someone to love and the recklessly open heart of the monk is available. He may do no more than smile at you or hold your hand for a second, but he is giving you what he has in the present moment to give you.

In the end, intimacy and companionship are different shades of the same color, and perhaps the distinctions we draw are false. What matters is that we open ourselves up and we love. What matters is that we love, every single gorgeous second we get a chance at it.

eight

The Making of a Heart—
It's Not Easy to Love

*I*t just isn't easy to love. People disappoint us when they are doing the best they can. None of us starts out in life mature, and none of us is automatically good at loving. It does seem that some are better at loving, naturally, than others. If we really look into their lives, we discover some special contributing factor that accounts for what seems like their "natural" ability to love. They may have helped care for their grandparents or had a handicapped sibling. Firstborn children of large families tend to be especially nurturing.

We need other people to help us grow. Sometimes it is the one who is most difficult to be around that we need the most. Sometimes we are the most difficult to be around, and then we need grace and acceptance. Without the defying and difficult presence of others we would not try as hard, because we would not have to. It is an inescapable reality that our relationships are the soil from which we grow a heart capable of caring.

Father Michael Green joined the monastery one year after Father Dan. They both grew up in Detroit and both went to the Benedictine high school. They knew each other in high school, casually. Their lives were both deeply touched by the monks, and forty years ago each of these young men left their home and family to go to St. Benedict Monastery. Dan is a year older than Mike. When the monastic community decided they needed these two young men to become priests, Dan went to Toronto to study theology a year before he was joined by Mike. Father Mike likes to say they actually majored in hockey.

While in Toronto, Father Dan started getting involved with teen ministry. He says he didn't know that the kids liked him. He was a quiet young man— not the kind of youth minister to wear orange pants, put a plant on his head, and dance on the table. At the end of his education, Dan returned home to

Michigan for his ordination and first mass. He was shocked—and delighted—when seven cars full of teens from Toronto showed up to celebrate his ordination. A celebration followed the great event. The events around his ordination were naturally very special to the newly ordained priest; he cherished that memory.

Something happened in Father Dan when those teenagers showed up. It revealed to him, in an undeniable way, that God was with him as he worked with youth. It confirmed his gift, and when our gifts and graces are confirmed we feel affirmed as a human being. That kind of thing is very special and we want to hold on to such an experience. We want to lock it in time and make it a defining moment.

His friend Mike was there, too. Father Mike is a gregarious kind of guy; he kisses all the women and babies in a room. One friend of Dan's says Father Mike reminds him of Tigger; you know Tigger, companion to Winnie the Pooh, who is "bouncy, trouncy . . . full of fun, fun, fun." That would be Father Mike. Whatever he does, he does with enthusiasm.

Father Mike and I were dance partners at a square-dance fundraiser a few years ago. If you've ever square danced, you know there is a move where the guy releases the woman's hand to another partner. It's a swing release kind of movement. He is supposed to release her and sort of step aside, then she moves in line with her next partner. It is intended to be a smooth move. However, with Father Mike, it was more like being launched than released—due to his energy and enthusiasm. That's Father Mike, full of fun, fun, fun.

One year after Dan's ordination, it was time for Mike to be ordained. Remember, there had been a celebration only a year previously during which Mike had become acquainted with Dan's young friends. For Father Mike, any friend of Father Dan's was a friend of his. It had been a lot of fun, and connections had been forged, so it was natural that Mike invited some of those young people to his party as well. It would also be their chance to see Father Dan again.

"I was furious," Dan recalls. "They were my friends, not his friends. How dare he invite my friends to his party? How dare he assume that would be fine with me—he did not even talk to me about it. In my anger, I wrote a letter to Mike. I told him to get his own friends. I told him he had no right to invite my friends. I said things I'm deeply ashamed of saying. I wrote the letter, shoved it under his door, and did I ever feel better. For a little while anyway."

Dan did not sleep much that night. By morning he was horrified at what he done. He was awake while Mike slept, peacefully happy with the events of the day. Dan could not believe he had given in to jealousy and pride. He couldn't believe he had said such awful things to his faithful friend. He was disgusted with himself.

Very early in the morning, after Dan had fallen into an exhausted sleep, Mike slipped the envelope back under Dan's door.

"He did an amazing thing. He returned the letter and wrote on the envelope, 'Dan, this isn't you.' It was the response I needed most, but could never have expected. He didn't just forgive me. He erased it and gave me the benefit of any doubt and he moved on, before we even discussed it. He actually did not even need to discuss it."

It was more grace than the young priest could have hoped for, and it has stuck with him all these years. When he thinks of the times he most needed grace, he most needed to be understood and forgiven, he remembers that one incident with Father Mike. It changed him and was part of the making of his heart for others. It reminded him that it's not easy to love even your oldest and best friend. Because Father Dan knows there are times when something that is less "real" in him sticks up its head, he is very understanding when it happens to other people.

His ability to understand is the product of monasticism. The life of the monk makes it difficult to avoid self. All that silence, solitude, and prayer puts you up close with who you really are. Living day after day with the same people you argued with last week and celebrated with last year—people who know your story—will keep your ideas about yourself in perspective. Sure, people can avoid themselves in monastic life. Any monk can tell you a story about how he has avoided himself and has seen others do it also. But their life in common, relentlessly in common, makes it tough to live out a pattern of self-avoidance.

All of us are hard to like and even harder to love sometimes. The human person is capable of great loyalty and great betrayal. One single, remarkable soul can house huge contradictions. You can't tell on the outside what is going on inside. From the moment we slip from the womb we begin the journey of becoming who we are. Even the best of childhoods traumatize our fragile souls and we learn to cover up and compensate.

We learn to clutch what is ours and we learn to mistrust others. There is always the real you. The one with the potential. The one you dream of becoming. The one you are in your best moments. As we grow spiritually, we recover this original identity and shed the many layers of the false self. This growth is an important part of spirituality.

Despite our complexities as human beings, there is no bad twin to blame when we behave like something less than human. It was not Father Dan's alter ego who wrote the nasty letter to his friend. But that action did emerge from a part of Dan that is fundamentally *not* the person he is becoming. Failure is not the final word, however. Even if we know that on an intellectual level, having someone affirm it the way Father Mike did for Father Dan helps tremendously.

You are becoming something. You are becoming more patient, more loving, but during the process you may discover that you are more angry, more inclined toward selfishness. Through the entire process, there is some fundamental person at the root of it all. It may be a person of love or a person of selfish indifference. Every day we make choices that take us toward the making of certain kind of heart. Who we become ends up being the accumulation of our choices to love or not.

We probably make most of our choices in favor of loving. However, it is rare to meet a person who makes all of their choices in favor of loving. Maybe the best we can do is to become more conscious of the choices and to try, really try, to love.

Hospitality is a way to help others discover their true selves. They need to see that precious person reflected in your eyes sometimes, before they can believe it for themselves. It is no easy thing to give this to other people. We know that. We can force ourselves, through gritted teeth and clenched spirits, to be gracious to the one who needs a second chance. Not much reward in it for us, but we know we can do it. We can let down our resistance and let acceptance happen naturally. It is better both for us and for the person.

Our ability to accept others begins with whether or not we are in touch with our dark side. As we have said, monks live with themselves without blinking at the dark side, and this is what allows them to be as accepting as they are. They are able to accept strangers without expecting them to be perfect.

You might remember a biblical story about a woman caught in adultery. Jesus tells the men who are about to stone her that the one who is without sin (and the Greek actually says "without this sin"—adultery) should toss the first stone. And he doesn't get any takers. Jesus doesn't seem surprised.

A realistic understanding of the self allows us to better accept others. If we can forgive ourselves, we become better at forgiving others. When we have searched hard for the best that is inside of ourselves, it becomes easier to find the best in others.

My youngest daughter, Andrea, was in an auto accident just before her seventeenth birthday. It was a near-fatal accident. You never forget sitting with a child in ICU, watching her chest move up and down, praying for every single breath. I thought of my daughter when I met a woman on an airplane who had been in an auto accident.

The woman was older than Andrea, and it appeared that her injuries were not as extensive. Her face had sustained a lot of damage, however. She wore the scars not only from the accident, but also from numerous reconstructive surgeries.

Usually, I read or sleep on flights. I'm not one to make small talk with other passengers. But this woman was determined to tell me her story. It was not a pretty story. The woman was angry and bitter. She had lost her face and no amount of surgery was going to give it back to her. She bragged about the Mercedes she bought with the insurance settlement money; she spoke of how she's "set for life" now. She even said that she has all the male attention she wants, despite being "ugly as sin" because she could always buy another "boy toy."

Not liking the direction of the conversation, I told her about my daughter and brought up the subject of anger and how people worked through anger after such a tragedy. It was not something the other woman wanted to discuss. Too bad for her, I thought. I'm not enjoying sitting beside you either, Lady.

In a similar situation, before Andrea's accident, I would have buried my nose in a book and not looked up, regardless of the woman's fervent attempts to attract my attention. I cherish my privacy. I didn't consider hospitality to include listening to annoying strangers on airplanes. I didn't have time for rude, angry people.

What made the difference? Gratitude. My own daughter had been spared. No one ever merits being spared; it isn't something you deserve or don't deserve. It is simply a gift. How could I not be grateful? Andrea was alive. Andrea was on a course toward healing and dealing with her rage. I knew people whose seventeen-year-old daughter had died in a car crash only a few years earlier. But Andrea would make it.

The woman next to me? Well, it was anyone's guess whether or not she would ever truly recover from the accident. And no amount of expensive cars or casual sex would change that reality. Was there anyone in the whole world who cared if she remained emotionally impaled by the accident? The woman didn't talk of family or friends—only things and people to be used.

What did it really cost me to listen? It was such a little thing, and it seemed that not many people had ever taken the time to do it. That was understandable; the woman was difficult to be around because she was self-centered, loud, and intent on being noticed. Without gratitude for my kid's life, it would have been very easy to ignore the woman.

Gratitude is at the center of a hospitable heart. It keeps everything in perspective. Often we allow day after gifted day to come and go without one sigh of gratitude for the beauty of it all. We don't slow our breath to hear the song of the wind or taste the miracle of an apple. We take for granted the health of the little ones who sleep in their beds, and we assume the one who loves me today will be here to love me again tomorrow. What an arrogant life we lead.

Perhaps you recall being thirteen and having someone tell you that you ought to be grateful that you have shoes because some people have no feet. Perhaps you recall being six and having your grandfather tell you that you ought to be grateful for liver and onions because some children go to bed hungry. You know, it did not make you feel grateful.

Knowing you should feel gratitude feels awful. It makes you feel rotten. Guilty. Like dirt. We know we ought to be grateful for every sunrise. We ought to be grateful for every bite of food. We ought to be grateful for every heart that has ever loved us. We ought to be grateful for every starry night. All of life is a resounding call to gratitude, and until we honestly feel the joy of gratitude, giving will be difficult for us.

Gratitude is the best and most honest feeling you will ever have. But you can't feel grateful just because you ought to.

Gratitude is what you feel on the perfect summer day with the wind in your face and the sun on your shoulder, as the laughter of someone you love kisses your ear. Try as hard as you know how, and still you can't do more than muster up a sense that yes, you ought to be grateful. You really cannot make it happen; gratitude, like faith, is given to you. It springs on you. It knocks the wind out of you just when everything seemed impossible. Anxiety makes you ready for gratitude. So does having enough courage not to dull the anxiety with alcohol, or spending, or eating, or whatever your usual escape might be. Shut the door, experience the anxiety, and you are ready for gratitude. You can't control gratitude or make it happen, regardless of what your mother told you. Try to force gratitude and you end up with guilt instead.

Gratitude happens most often during suffering, loss, and other really hard stuff. It is the leading edge of joy. It happens when the big reality hits you. You have no more right to be loved than anyone else. Your job is a fluke. Your children have no more right to health and security than the children in Bosnia. Your friends are not obligated to put up with you. Your education—well, consider yourself fortunate you were not born into the poverty of Calcutta. It is all a gift. Every single molecule, every smile, every taste of sunshine is a gift.

Gratitude opens up space inside of us for others. There is less of me in me when I am grateful. I can see that you, too, are a gift to me. Even if you aren't easy to be around. There was a monk who lived with Father Dan at the monastery for many years. He is gone now, no longer a monk, but during his stay he was the most difficult to live with of any monk, or any person, Father Dan had ever known.

The monk took no responsibility for his actions, his emotions, or his boatload of dysfunction. Plus, he never got the idea of community. If something went wrong, he pointed out how it was someone else's fault. He left little doubt that he was out solely for himself. He did no more than he had to do. If he was sweeping the kitchen and you asked him to sweep the pantry too, he would say, "It isn't my job to sweep the pantry." He was the kind who took the last piece of apple pie without asking if anyone would like to share it with him. He was suspicious of all the monks, saying that some of them went into his room when he was away and took things from him.

Day after day, Dan looked across the table at this annoying man and faced the reality of looking across the table at him for the rest of his life. How can we be anything but a stranger to someone so thoroughly impossible to like?

Dan says he never did learn to like the monk, but while he was Prior he had the sacred responsibility to look after the monk's growth. He encouraged him to become involved with needy people. Father Dan hoped that compassion would incite growth. He encouraged him to use his gifts to work with others. Dan insisted that the monk try new things and attempt to open his mind to new possibilities. Dan persevered in his attempts to find the real person behind all the negativity. It was a difficult situation for both Prior and monk. But the man seemed to be in love with his own destruction. He refused to listen, and above all a monk must listen.

"I can get along with almost anyone. I have never been more challenged to accept someone than I was with that particular monk," Father Dan remembers. He admits that frequently monks struggle to understand and accept each other; it does not happen automatically. Perseverance with the unlovable one will often hold you until a breakthrough occurs. Sometimes, however, the breakthrough never comes. It never came with the monk, and he eventually left.

Dan knows, however, that it was good for him, personally, to struggle and keep trying. He had no way to avoid the man and had to be open to the notion that God had brought them both to the monastery at the same time to live a shared life.

We all have rough edges that need some sanding down. Everyone is a bag of contradictions. Usually we are not in such bad shape emotionally that others flee from us, but we are still contrary and difficult sometimes. Trying to find the good in others, and working with them to reveal it, helps soften us around the edges.

What is the secret of people who seem always to feel grateful without being prompted, people who keep looking for the good in others, those who welcome others even when it is hard to do?

These people have courage. Courage takes us past thinking and talking about hospitality into the realm of the will. Courage is the power of the heart, and it resides not in the emotion, but in the will and the power to choose. Courageous people will themselves to move past an obstacle that paralyzes others.

Remember *The Wizard of Oz?*

It is the story of Dorothy, who is trying to get home. Dorothy does not lack courage. She's lost, but she is not cowardly. The Tin Man thinks he lacks a heart, and the Scarecrow thinks he lacks a brain, and the Cowardly Lion thinks he lacks courage—only the Lion is right; what they all lack, we eventually find out, is courage. They lack the courage to become more than they are. They lack the courage to get through the tough times, and when they stand in the hall of mirrors and smoke and roaring voices they lack the courage to declare themselves—all except the little girl, who has come this far by courage and will make it home by courage.

One day Father Mike and I were working on the monastery computers when a rude and uninvited visitor showed up. It was during the period that the monastery's chapel was under construction. We had been at work for a couple hours when a young man suddenly walked into the room. Father Mike asked him who he was and what he wanted. He was pointed without being rude.

The man told Mike that the person who was using the scaffolding outside had rented it from him and had not made payments, and so he was there to take it down and take it home. He said that he had called the guy's wife and the guy's mother, and no one was giving him any satisfaction. As he talked, the visitor grew more agitated. His hands hung clenched at his sides. He was taking on the appearance of someone looking for a fight. "No one screws me," he said loudly, as if it were Father Mike who owed him for the scaffolding.

Mike suggested they talk about it in the hallway. He wanted to make sure I was out of the line of fire if things got out of hand. The man just continued to rant, finally saying, "I am going to take the scaffolding and you can't stop me!"

Father Mike replied, "I'm not going to try and stop you, but neither am I giving you permission to take it. All I've heard is your side of the story, and there is bound to be more to it than what you have told me. If you have decided you are taking the scaffolding, then just go do it, but remember, I am not allowing you to take it. You are removing it from our property without my permission."

Mike was firm and clear. He kept his voice low and he looked the man in the eye steadily. He refrained from matching the man anger for anger, insult for insult. His was the voice of reason.

Despite Mike's concern for the monastery and the person with him, despite his anxiety over what this man might do next, Mike kept a cool head. He was not intimidated by the huff and gruff of a bully. He knew that what stood before him was a scared little man making a lot of noise, bellowing and blowing hot air.

Father Mike was courageous. He did not back down. He did not give in. He did not compromise. He remained respectful while being appropriately strong. His calm, steady reply drained the hot air from the unexpected visitor. When Mike finished, the man stood there a moment, his legs apart, his arms folded in a defensive stance. He said again, "You can't stop me."

Mike paused and said, "I'm not trying to stop you."

The man turned and left the room. He had come looking for a fight. He was so angry with the man to whom he had rented the equipment that he arrived on the work site ready to do battle. He was set to fight the first person he encountered. But Father Mike did not need to do battle. He had nothing to prove.

It is important that we not allow people to drag us into their fights with the world. We have to stay on the outside of the situation and attempt to discern what is really happening. Do they want the problem resolved, or are they just looking for a fight?

The difficult person comes with a mountain of emotion attached. The emotion itself can become the center of any relating that happens. We are not doing the person any good if we become caught up in their emotion and negativity.

If we center down into the quiet in our hearts, we can hear what is really happening. As we grow in meditation and prayer, we become better at resting in the center. When you are conscious of living every second gathered before the divine you just do not rattle easily. Father Mike has spent over forty years at prayer. He has the ability to see who a person really is. He is able to discern what is actually happening in a certain situation.

When Dan tells us of how Mike forgave him because "that wasn't really you," and we hear of how Mike dealt with a confrontational hothead, we hear in both stories an ability to size up a situation and get to the heart of it, quickly. You aren't born with that ability. It comes only through years of paying attention to people, listening to them and hearing the sounds of a human heart being the most honest it knows how to be.

When you hear that sound, you don't forget it; you recognize it afterward every single time it happens. But you will not hear it at all if you don't pay attention to people. If I am the stranger attempting to be known, and there you are, not listening, will I keep trying? Probably not. As hard as it is, try to hear the one who is hard to love.

"Because how can we be other than strangers when at those rare moments of our lives when we stop hiding from each other and try instead passionately and profoundly to make ourselves known to each other, we find this is precisely what we cannot do?" wonders writer Frederick Buechner in *Telling Secrets*.

When we relate to a difficult person, we operate from a basic assumption: I need to protect myself. But to live the way of hospitality means extending grace to people. You cannot be hospitable and gracious from behind your high wall. If you live by grace you become helpful. You become accepting. Even when it is impossible to accept certain behaviors and impossible to like them, you accept them. The centrality of love insists that we give the hard-to-like a chance.

Of course the difficulty of loving is complicated. It is not only the hard-to-like that we have trouble accepting; it is everyone. It is just hard to love sometimes.

"I honestly want to be more open to people, but I face people and situations that make it impossible."

"Yes, I want to be more hospitable, but I see no reason why I should open up to people who will use me and be ungrateful for what they are given."

"I know that Jesus went around accepting people and associating with the outcasts, but Jesus didn't live in the world I live in."

"I would love you, but you really are not all that lovable."

But.

The word *but* is all about our doubts, our justifications, and our excuses. To stop accepting your own excuses is a very courageous act.

We need time and practice to grow in accepting the difficult people. We must try or it will never happen at all. Hidden at the heart of all Creation is an original goodness. If we live in the presence of the Divine through prayer and gratitude, if we live courageously, this goodness will reveal itself.

It is very hard to keep a straight face and say there is good in everyone. We have seen evidence to the contrary, haven't we? It is hard to believe, but we keep trying to prove that there is good in everyone. We know people don't always choose goodness. We only have to look in the mirror to be reminded of that.

Goodness, most of the time, seems like an impossible dream, and the quest to find it in others no more than the fantasy of children. But if we don't try to believe it, we will end up densely fatalistic and unable to see the most obvious good. It is worth the effort to believe.

We give each other another chance to make the right choice when we accept and forgive, even when it is very difficult. Hospitality to the unchosen goodness in others will come more easily if we are practicing with ourselves.

Our ability to care is more than we know. Prayer will expand it. Courage will expand it. Risk will expand it. Caring, the tiny little bit of it we can manage, will expand as we give ourselves more chances to say yes to others.

In the Disney animated movie *Lion King*, there is a scene in which the adolescent Simba comes to the end of his running from himself. He has escaped, hidden, and taken on an attitude that nothing matters. As he is chased down by the truth about himself, his Father appears to him and says, "You are more than you have become."

Regardless of what you and I have become, regardless of what anyone has become—we are all created to be more. There is an unchosen goodness in us. It exists, whether or not we choose it. We must learn to make the choices that will make us more.

This is the Christian story, the dominant story that guides the Western world. Jesus always called people to more. He called them beyond their plans for themselves, beyond their religious convictions, beyond their conditions. We can call each other beyond our worst choices and darkest moments.

nine

Making Room for Yourself

*I*t is impossible to address the topic of hospitality without considering an individual's rights and boundaries. In pop psychology the word *boundaries* is used to describe the lines we each draw to protect ourselves. Psychologists consistently agree that individuals require some boundaries for a full and healthy life.

A few years ago my husband, David, and I welcomed into our home a man who had just been released from prison. He was a friend of my brother, and he had nowhere else to go. The family he came from had not taught him to respect other people or to insist that others respect you. The real meaning of *boundaries* is the insistence that I will not be violated by your selfishness.

If he had any fragile sense of boundaries, prison destroyed all of them. When he arrived in our household he had no idea when it was appropriate to enter a conversation, he did not know when and how to the use the phone in a way that respected other people, he said the wrong thing at the wrong time, he did not knock on doors when he should, and he was too meek in other situations. He had no sense of boundaries.

It was disturbing. One night, very late, I heard him on the telephone with a woman he was dating. He wasn't quite screaming, but he wasn't using his inside voice either. He was also using language I didn't appreciate waking up to in the middle of the night.

I went into the kitchen where he was on the phone and pacing. I stood in his path and said, "Your conversation is over now. Hang up the phone and go back to bed. Never do this again or I will have to hurt you." No, I had no actual intention of harming him, it was hyperbole, yet there were actual consequences he could incur at my hand—and he knew it.

He didn't do it again. He knew that I won't have my boundaries trampled all over. I would continue to try to be understanding—but he was going to act in a respectful manner, whether he felt respect or not.

His presence was an interesting comparison to one of the monk who has a very well-managed full set of boundaries. At the time, I was researching a writing project and had mentioned it to my friend Brother Damien (now Father Damien). He was in seminary. He suggested I visit the library on campus, because he thought I'd find the specific collection of theological journals I required.

He offered to take me to campus with him. I could research in the morning and then we would take a walk around campus and have lunch, he suggested.

On campus were a couple of things he was sure I would enjoy seeing—the chapel, for example, and the grounds that are lovely to walk. While in the library, I noticed him stick his head in the door and locate me between classes, just to check on me. He never approached or interrupted my work. He was comfortable enough to give me space and to leave it to me to decide when I was ready to see the chapel and when we would walk the campus. He could not have been more respectful of my boundaries. He was a fascinating contrast to our houseguest. The contrast became even clearer over lunch.

Damien ordered an egg dish with vegetables, no meat. He was very clear when he ordered. His lunch arrived jammed with ham. It was Lent, and he had given up meat for Lent. He looked at the steaming dish in front of him and said, "If this passes my lips— it's over," and he made a slicing motion at his neck. I laughed and asked if the execution of monks over Lenten offenses was a new monastery policy.

He called back the waitress and insisted that she take it back and bring him what he had ordered. He wanted a new entrée; they were not merely to remove the ham from this one. Father Damien has worked in food service running a family restaurant. He took the word *service* very seriously. Incompetence in service, a lack of consideration for the people you serve, the failure to respect the clear wishes and needs of others—all of these were simply unacceptable. Damien has well-established boundaries. He will not allow others to violate him, yet he is one of the most open and giving people you could ever meet.

Being a person with strong and wise boundaries does not make you selfish. It is refusing to let others have boundaries that makes you selfish; it is insisting that others must make *you* the center of their lives that is selfish.

Maintaining boundaries is how we remain hospitable and accepting of ourselves. I said earlier that none of us will ever have a better relationship with another human being than the one we have with ourselves. One way to nurture a healthy sense of the self is to keep strong boundaries. People who like themselves tend to maintain boundaries quite naturally.

While it is important that we remain open and available, none of us is a public place either. Denying what we really and truly need, in some misunderstood notion about being hospitable toward others or being loving toward others, is simply bad for you. You need time to yourself. You need respect.

Boundaries allow us to give more to others, not less. Boundaries do not exclude the other; in fact, if you become a person with actual boundaries, you are better able to give to other people because you do not feel diminished by it. Giving is a joy because you want to give, and not because someone has manipulated you and you gave in.

Boundaries keep us from feeling used or manipulated. When we set perimeters and refuse to allow ourselves or others to be violated, we become free to enjoy giving. We become free to experience a certain glee in giving joy to others.

A few years ago, after the publication of our first book, our editor was visiting the monastery with his wife. The editor, a close friend, happened to work for an old, very respected Catholic press. Father Thomas, a monk visiting from Sri Lanka, absolutely loved that Catholic press. He considered anything they published to be next in authority only to Rome. As much as Dan liked the editor, he didn't agree with Father Thomas. But he saw an opportunity to give a great deal of joy to his brother monk.

After mass, I wanted to introduce Father Dan to the editor's wife, but he was nowhere to be found among the coffee-drinking guests rubbing shoulders in the monk's living room. Most of the monks spent time with their visitors making conversation, drinking coffee, and eating doughnuts. Dan was usually included in that number. Father Thomas, being quite shy, usually went to his room and did not mix with the guests. If you caught him alone, he was delighted to talk to you, but he didn't do crowds very well.

Our guests were at my side, but still no Father Dan in sight, when suddenly there was Father Thomas heading straight toward us, beaming like a silly kid who got what he wanted for Christmas. The reserved, noble monk was actually animated, almost bouncy, something I had never seen before.

He smiled at me and reached for the hands of our guests. He just kept shaking the hand of the tall, quiet editor, who was by then wearing a wide grin. You can't imagine how out of character this was for the monk from Sri Lanka. He shook the editor's hand, he talked, he commended him with booming enthusiasm. Meeting someone from such a highly esteemed Catholic press was sheer delight for Father Thomas, something he could have never expected. A moment he would never forget. My editor and friend had no idea he was such a celebrity.

Moments later, Dan's hand descended on my shoulder as he joined us. He had obviously gone to Father Thomas and told him the identity of the guest. Then he changed from his habit and joined the fun, enjoying with a twinkle in his eye every moment that Father Thomas beamed at the editor while vigorously and endlessly shaking the man's hand. Father Dan had set up Father Thomas for joy.

Hospitality will give the other a handful of joy, if it's possible to do, and that kind of hospitality gives you more bliss than you've given someone else. It is a good reminder that hospitality does not violate you; it doesn't mean you have to be a martyr. Instead it can make you very happy. But you can't give yourself to others when there is no clear sense of a self.

The monk is under constant pressure today to be more available to those outside of the monastery. Just as you are not a public place, neither is a monastery. Wouldn't you think that would be clear?

It isn't. Dan can tell dozens of stories about intruders who walk in as if the monastery were a public library, right into the monk's living space. These aren't friends of the monks; they are more like tourists who want a picture of a monk.

The monastery has had a longstanding, recurring problem with teenagers coming to the monastery in the middle of the night to rip up the grass by spinning their car tires and to chase each other through the woods. Sometimes these teenagers have gone so far as to enter the retreat house or the monastery.

They come from a nearby small city where students have passed around a story about the monks from one class to the next. The rumor they tell is that the monks are dangerous devilish men who perform evil rites, hold people captive, and chase innocent teenagers through the woods with knives and axes. Makes you think they've watched too many bad movies.

The monks and retreatants have been the targets of vandalism, gunshots, and much unacceptable, old-fashioned rudeness. Dan says they have tried everything to combat these problems. They invite the students into the retreat so they can see what is going on, hoping they will understand. They don't; they only cause trouble. The monks have become adept at rounding up the kids and hauling them inside the retreat house for lecturing and scolding until the police arrive.

"We've tried reasoning with them, we've tried threatening them with the local police, we've called their parents. The sheer nerve of these kids infuriates me. They think nothing of entering our property for the purposes of destruction, violation, and stirring up trouble," Dan says.

Father Dan has given interviews to the high school newspaper in that little city, explaining who the Benedictine monks are and what they are doing with all those teenagers in the retreat house. He has hoped that information would end the stupidity.

Finally, the monks put up high gates and locked them. They found no other solution to the problem. This is what every person with a healthy sense of self does at times. We lock out the threat. We refuse to let the destructive thing come close. When hospitality to others becomes destructive, the healthiest emotional and spiritual response is to forbid or impede access, even though it can be heartbreaking. Especially if it means ending a relationship you valued.

The monks cannot hold to their way of life if they overlook the monastic requirement for some cloistered space, some separation and silence. To be fully present to the guest, they must continue, first of all, to be monks. They cannot lose their distinction as Benedictines. This has become increasingly challenging for them as the public has appeared at their chapel, in their walkways, and wandering the paths around the monastery.

You, too, will wrestle with issues of privacy and personal space. You have commitments to keep, and these commitments shape your life. You dishonor yourself, and the people who love you, if you fail to keep your commitments while chasing after a spiritual ideal such as hospitality.

Becoming a hospitable person and keeping your life in balance are not without complications. Monasticism is a gift to the world only as it keeps its distinction. You're also distinctive. You must remain who you are and allow yourself to grow more yourself every day. Hospitality will help that happen—it is one of many things that will help that happen—but you must remain freely yourself. If you lose your distinctiveness, the world has lost something it will never see again—you.

Words like *accepting* and *allowing* are a bit misleading. They suggest passivity, as if you are going to become more yourself by doing nothing, and that isn't so. You walk the line between insisting on your right to be yourself, and doing nothing, to become more real. It's the same struggle the monks face. They must not lose who they are—that would be a monstrous loss to the entire world—but neither can they live in isolation.

The part of us that we give to others, to the stranger you might say, is our outer self. Saying it is an outer self does not mean it is false or superficial. It means we reserve our most sacred inner places for those who are trusted to walk gently with us on that soil.

With the outer self we give attention. We listen. We offer genuine concern and attempt to enter the experience of someone else. We appreciate the person, and give them something of ourselves, without expecting them to become a friend. We don't necessarily share secrets, inner feelings, dreams, or ambitions and passions.

What we do in hospitality is very important. It does not lessen its importance to admit that it does not always go soul deep, because neither is it shallow. The simple courtesy of looking strangers in the eye affirms people. When strangers talk to you they are saying, "Hey, I'm here, I matter, pay attention to me." You build up their humanity when you pay attention.

What does go soul deep is how these seemingly casual encounters of graciousness with others affect you and affect them. They fill the very deep need of the human heart to be heard.

While visiting the monastery I've sometimes had a grandchild or two along. Gina began calling Father Dan "Grampa Dan" when she was two "because he looks more like a grampa than a father," she reasoned. She has been known to say, "Hi, Grampa Dan!" regardless of where we are or who is in earshot.

One afternoon Dan and I were working on a book project and paying not enough attention to the two-year-old Gina. She was climbing up and down the steps in the retreat house and checking out the bedrooms, as we worked. Suddenly the child had our attention as she yelled, "Look at me, look at me, look at me . . ." while bolting up and down like a spring, her arms flapping and ponytail swinging. Enough with the ignoring a cute kid, she was saying. Look over here. Inside, most of us still live like a two-year-old calling out, "Look at me."

It can be emotionally draining to give yourself to someone who has the neediness of a child. These are the people who are most likely to push against your boundaries, and they rarely have boundaries of their own. They are also the most in need of a simple gesture of acceptance.

A couple years ago, after the publication of *Benedict's Way: An Ancient Monk's Insights for a Balanced Life*, a reporter from a local radio station wanted to interview Dan and me. She came for a preliminary interview. We had given a number of interviews by then and had it down to a system. But, I had to tell Dan this one might be different.

The other woman and I were once news editors at competing stations, years earlier. It had grown ugly a couple times and the woman had come to loathe me. She was insecure, I explained to Dan. She never quite understood that when I scooped her on a story, it wasn't personal. I hoped the other woman had put it in the past.

We were only a few minutes into the interview when it became clear that something was very wrong with the reporter. She asked *us* what questions she should ask, then her gaze jerked toward Father Dan's face, but utterly avoided looking at me. The journalist giggled at the wrong time, when talking about a tragedy, and then said, "I do know that's not funny. It's a nervous giggle," she admitted.

When she took our picture for the website, she asked us to look at her. She then said to Dan (presumably because he's male), "I know I'm hard to look at but you'll have to try," and then giggled again. She was falling apart with each passing moment. Her hands shook and her painful awkwardness was excruciating to watch. At one point, Dan looked at me and clutched my hand in a silent, "We have to do something!" I glared at him and shook off his hand. The woman, after all these years, was still annoying.

The reporter finally brought up our past, admitting that we had not liked each other. I did not tell her I had actually been indifferent, but agreed it was true. Pushing aside annoyance, I said, "It was a very long time ago. We were young journalists. I think we're both different people now." She looked startled and fumbled with her camera, dropping things. As Dan helped her, I said, "We both are doing things we love now aren't we? Really, there's nothing to be concerned about."

Despite my best attempts, things did not improve. She continued to fall apart as if something about the situation was rocking her to the core. Dan wanted to reach out. After years of friendship I could spot the signs. He wanted her to understand that she mattered. He reached out to her suffering, while hospitable me became deeply annoyed with what I considered her immaturity.

I remember the softening of his eyes as he listened to her, the change in his body language as he tried to reassure her. The kind of caring he wanted to extend to her is typical in hospitality. He was not trying to be her new best friend. He was simply being kind. She had a story of great pain and rejection. Not that she wasn't a neurotic mess—truly she was—but not without good reason.

People do not need much from us. Actually, they require very little—simple caring really—yet that seems to be more than we have to give. Yes, to be available to those who are needy can cost us emotionally, but we do not offer them our deepest self. If we protect ourselves with appropriate boundaries, we are not threatened by this needy kind of person because they so happily receive whatever little we can give.

We give to meet a need, but giving also soothes our own wounds. You like yourself better after you've reached out to someone like that reporter. Kindness and acceptance are basic to human nature; we need them like we need water and air. We will become less if we don't give it, if we don't receive it. You and I can give a great big bunch of kindness without even coming close to violating boundaries.

Opening up to others does not mean you tolerate disrespect or harm to yourself. It does not mean you let people rip chunks off of you. It does not mean you cease to take care of yourself or do what you need to do to remain emotionally, physically, and spiritually healthy. We can give simple kindness without losing ourselves.

ten

Being a Companion Through the Hurt

*L*ife can be deeply painful. No surprise, right? One of the most important ways of extending hospitality is to quietly companion the person who is going through some awful thing. It is no easy thing to be available to the one who is suffering a pain you can't relieve.

My first, and at the time only, child was dying of cancer when I was twenty years old. Angie's battle had been a short one. At four and a half months the cancer was discovered—she had a tumor on her shoulder—and a mere six months later she was days away from death. In her last days people found it excruciating to be near her, which I understood. At times, if there had been a way for me to escape I would have taken it.

Many people wanted to help, however—at least they believed they did. I never doubted their sincerity. Who could resist the tiny, dark-haired baby with huge eyes and a startling ethereal kind of beauty? She was born Christmas Eve and there had been something special about the child from the first day. Lots of people commented on it. Being in a room with her made you feel better. Angela soon became Angel to many people.

Because so many were offering to help, a friend of the family organized a schedule, intending that the baby and I not be left alone in those final frightful days. People signed up for shifts that were supposed to last from two hours to overnight. It was the rare person who lasted a whole night.

Angela was in terrible pain, pain like someone had dropped an anvil on her arm. She was prescribed pain medication to take every four hours to ease the suffering, and the medication did help—a little. About two hours after the dose she would grow restless and begin whimpering. Walking with her, holding her, singing to her, worked to quiet her and comfort her at this point.

At about two and a half hours she could not be comforted and did not want to be held. She would lie in her crib and throw her head back and forth, her mouth open, often with no sound coming out, as if the pain could not be expressed.

At three hours, she started screaming and trying to rock from side to side in the crib while still lying on her back. No caretaker ever made it past three hours before administering more medication. The baby would calm down, often sleep. But you always knew the crying was coming again. You always knew nothing would prevent the onslaught of more pain for the infant.

If the crying didn't get you, the tumor did. She was not a large baby. The tumor on her little shoulder was the size of a large man's fist where it had broken through her china-doll skin. Though bandaged, it wept blood and water constantly. Her arm was engorged to the point of being useless, so when you held her, you had to prop up her arm on your shoulder or support it for her.

People avoided her. We don't deal with the hard realities, such as beautiful children suffering, unless we are forced to. We get through life with some peace of mind by not looking at the hungry children, the dying children, the bombed children, the kids with black eyes and cigarette burns on their legs. It takes a whole lot of courage to do otherwise. In the last few days of my daughter's life a courageous stranger came to stay with us.

I didn't really know Linda very well. She was the pastor's wife at a little conservative church one of my friends attended. They were the kind that were rather noisy about their "born again" religion. I used to tell my friend that while she had a personal savior, I had the same one everyone else had and he was enough. As you can imagine, I wasn't sure having Linda over to help out would work. I imagined her leaving religious materials in my bathroom and scolding me for not praying long enough or hard enough.

But that wasn't Linda. People are always better than the stereotype we try to stuff them into. She had a son who was only weeks older than Angela. Linda showed up one day and she stayed. She made tea and she cooked beef stew. She washed the sheets on all the beds and she handed me a sleeping pill.

Baby clothes didn't fit Angela very well with the huge tumor and engorged arm. The seam of the right sleeve had to be cut open to make her clothing fit. There were a lot of cute little outfits with ripped seams, cute little outfits given as gifts from my mother and grandmother who had dreams for the life of this precious grandbaby.

Linda was with me when I had to rip the strong seam of a new garment given to us by my grandmother. The ripping of the seam matched the ripping in my heart, and as it opened up, so did the deep well of anger and hurt and confusion inside of me. Linda held me as the emotional dam ruptured and flooded us both. .

In my mind, Linda is forever framed by the screen door at the back of my little house. I can still see her standing there, trying to make sense of it all, trying to understand what this child's awful suffering said about the world and the God she loved. She had been with us for forty-eight hours. She would remain with me, even after Angela died, until my spouse, who was in the Armed Forces, and family could get there to be with me. Then she would disappear back to her life and I would never see her again.

That night she looked out into the unseasonably warm October night and said in a shaky voice, "I don't understand why God allows children to suffer like this. I don't know why this is happening and what it means. But I know this: You can trust a God who bleeds.

When you can't trust anything else, you can trust a God who bleeds."

She said the words out loud, but I had the definite impression Linda was talking to herself, rather than me. Linda's primary Christian image was of a God who gave himself and held nothing back from his Creation, a God who died with the cost of loving. Her availability to us, strangers she considered her sisters in Christ, grew naturally out of her deep faith.

Linda stood beside me during the darkest time of my life. She opened her heart knowing for sure it was going to get broken. Being with us would force her to look right into the face of realities and doubts she had been able to avoid, until she held the dying baby and thought of her own son. In becoming available to us, she paid a high price emotionally and spiritually.

I don't know how I would have survived without Linda. She became the face of God to me when God seemed gone. I could not find a way to pray or believe in a good God. I could not get past the anger and doubt, but I could hold on to this woman. I wasn't sure how to take the next breath, but I could take her love and feel her love. I didn't have to give back anything. Good thing, because I wasn't capable of it. I could let her take care of us. It was the hardest time I've ever known and during it, God's name was Linda.

During the national memorial service to honor those lost in the September 11, 2001, attacks, there was a woman who prayed a televised prayer, "God give us a sign that you're still here."

The sign that God is still here is the goodness we rediscovered in one another. God was still here when people escorted Muslim mothers and children on their daily errands. These were some of the signs that God remained with us.

"We are here to be God's presence to you," is what a bishop said to a grieving family at a funeral recently. When people are bent over with the weight of suffering, they need from us only our presence. If we give them that, truly give them that, we become for them the presence of God in a most tangible way. That is hospitality.

The situation does not have to be as dramatic as what happened with Linda. Few of us will ever be involved in such a life-shattering situation. But we can be present in everyday ways to those who hurt and those who are shunned. We can make a pot of chili and take it to a single mother or offer to babysit for a single father. We can mow the grass of the man who is recovering from heart surgery, or play checkers with the old woman who has cancer and will not last another month.

There is no shortage of pain you can relieve. But you know, just as Linda knew, that it is going to be costly. You will barely escape with your own self. And, whatever sense of self and the world you get out with, it will never be the same. You can't engage with human pain and remain unchanged. But that is the beauty of it. It will cost you everything and you will gain everything.

When we say we become God's presence and that something beautiful emerges from the suffering, we aren't saying that God makes these things happen so that we will reap these results, like benefits in some nightmarish cosmic insurance policy. Events happen because freedom allows events to happen; they happen on their own, and the randomness of it all can be heart stopping. God is present in the awful thing—not as its origin, but as the One who even in the most skin-crawling and torturous of events, offers the miraculous possibility of healing and a new beginning.

In his book *Voices of Silence*, Frank Bianco tells the story of Bede, a rather stuck-in-a-rut Trappist monk. It was in the post–Vatican II days, when monasteries all over the country were struggling to find ways to be more open to laity. This particular monk was against such a thing.

"There will be women in shorts running around," he grumbled. He had gone to the monastery to avoid women in shorts. But he couldn't stop the strong hand of the Spirit throwing open locked doors in those days, and the laity and the women showed up.

One day Bede was praying in the chapel. From behind him, in the area roped off for visitors, he heard a young woman crying. Her cry pierced his brittle heart, and before he knew what he was doing, he was heading toward the area roped off for visitors. When he reached the velvet cord, he grabbed it almost in anger. He knew now that love was never meant to be bound. Unhooking the rope, he half-flung it to the floor and moved toward the pew.

The young woman who sat there had not heard him approaching. "Please," he asked, "is there anything I can do?"

She looked up into his face, seeing what she would later describe as an exact copy of her father's face, only older. Her father had cancer and she feared for his life. The father she adored might soon be gone. She did not know how she would live the rest of her life without him. She hated how the cancer was hurting him.

The monk soon discovered that the young woman was his granddaughter, which neither the monk nor the girl had known. He had been in a relationship and had intended to marry a young woman before World War II, but had gone off to war. While he was gone her family had forbidden her to marry him. She was expecting a child by then—his son. He went straight from the war to the monastery without ever looking back.

Bede did not know his son was looking for him and believed he was in a monastery in Massachusetts (Bede was actually in Kentucky). Then, the son received a call from his daughter saying she had met a monk "who could easily be your twin if you were twenty years older."

If the monk had kept his heart clenched, he would never have known his granddaughter and would not have been able to be with his son, nursing him back to health. Bede died in a car accident shortly after returning to the monastery following his leave of absence. He had to overcome all his worst fears to get past the ropes that kept the suffering girl at a distance. Once he got past the barriers there was no turning back; everything was different. Do you think he ever regretted it?

In taking on the pain of others we act in the transformation of the world. We ourselves are changed, and we make a small push against the darkness. We make a difference. Benedict wanted his monks to make a difference.

We can be hospitable to others in very ordinary ways. When we are companions through the hurt, chances are it will cost us emotionally. If we care for the dying, eventually we'll lose our hearts to someone who is dying. If we work in a shelter for battered women and their children, one day someone will get through the thickest of skin. We can't feed the hungry without asking the hard questions about why there is hunger. This kind of hospitality will extract everything from us, leaving us stripped of our pretty delusions.

Through the years a lot of young people have taken their broken dreams and disheveled young lives to Subiaco Retreat House at St. Benedict Monastery for repair. Not long ago the monks found a young woman in their chapel who had been on retreat at the monastery in her teens. It turned out that she had gone into the dark, empty retreat house the night before and slept in one of the bedrooms. Like many young adults she had gone home for the holidays. But the difference with her was that her mother didn't want her home. The girl just wanted to be near the place she still considered home, so she returned anyway and ended up at the monastery.

The young woman's family story is one of the worst you can imagine. During some of the worst times of her teen years she had sat on one of the big rocks lining the monastery driveway. She felt safe there, welcome, and loved. She felt like the world made some sense.

Through tears she told the monks, "I just had to come back and sit on my rock and sleep in the retreat house again." Father Dan says this happens more than he ever imagined it would.

It is not unusual that when life becomes strained and confusing, the former teen retreatants, now in their twenties and thirties, head back to a place where they felt sheltered. Some of the former teens stay in touch and become friends of the monastery. Others just reappear one day in profound emotional distress. A while back, one young man showed up in such a state. He wanted to see both Father Dan and Mary Cummings. There was no way that was possible without him joining the teen retreat, even though the man was closing in on thirty years old.

"Neither of us minded," Dan said. "We knew from experience that his presence was going to complicate things, though. He would need attention from us and it would be emotionally exhausting. We needed to be at our strongest for the teens on retreat. It wasn't the first time such a thing had happened. We thought we knew what to expect." He said they could not have prepared themselves for how far into despair the man had tumbled. His emotional state required that one of them be with him, almost constantly. Both Dan and Mary were afraid he would hurt himself if left alone. Throughout the weekend, they took shifts being with the teens and being with the man curled up with his pain in a back bedroom.

During the visit, this friend attended the Office of Prayer with the monks. One night at Vespers he began sobbing. His whole body shook, and it was clear that something had broken and was now available for healing.

"We were at Vespers, our evening prayer, and we were standing while chanting. The whole time he was sobbing, we kept chanting and praying. You could almost see the prayer wrapping around him, surrounding him with strength and righting something inside of him that needed righting. While it was very tempting, every monk there knew it was the wrong time to take him aside and question him or attempt to comfort him. Instead, we did what we monks do. We kept our hand to the task and we prayed. In what is ordinary to us, his healing began."

It is the ordinary things we do to care for others that will make a difference in the most difficult of situations. Suffering is inconvenient. It alters our plans. It takes a swipe at us when we are not looking. None of us likes or welcomes the sudden interruption or change that alters everything.

But hospitality is not a planned event or a series of routine gestures. It is the stance of the heart that is abandoned to love. In monasticism, this ability to remain open to the other is fed by the monastic vow of stability.

For practical purposes the vow of stability has to do with staying physically in one place. A Benedictine monk can expect to live his life and die in one place—the monastery. There is a singleness of purpose to a life of stability; some questions are resolved once and for all. Stability is harder to come by if you have not taken a vow.

Change is the constant that most people live with and expect. Because any interruption in the course of events is just another change in a long line of interruptions and changes, we sometimes find it difficult to welcome the interruption. We so much want to lay plans and have them work. The seeming randomness of the universe leaves us feeling helpless, so we grasp at control.

One way to come to terms with these kinds of interruptions is to clean up as many loose ends in your life as you can. You will feel more relaxed and able to be with someone when you are not scooting through the day in fifteen-minute increments. Don't over-plan your day. Cut your schedule to as few activities as possible. Keep it simple, and plan to be interrupted.

Every person we know has more than enough of everything. Another way to free up time and give the soul a chance to relax is to unload some of the stuff you've collected. If all you do is dust it, maybe it should find another home. There is nothing wrong with owning and enjoying. But sometimes we forget that enough is enough.

If you have not worn it for a couple years, give it to someone who will wear it. If you have not read it, viewed it, listened to it anytime recently, why store it and dust it? What we accumulate gets inside of us. Life is enough to manage without having to manage so much irrelevant stuff too. Simplify. Now be careful about this. You can also complicate simplification. Dozens of books exist on the subject, and you can even attend conferences on how to simplify. Fine, if it helps. Most people can simplify life by just being honest with themselves and deciding what matters most.

In addition to simplifying as much as possible, making promises and keeping promises will free us to be more open to others. Commitment brings with it a great deal of freedom because, by its nature, it closes down options. We have become a people of too many options. Really now, how many brands of shampoo does one nation need?

Commitment can do for us what stability does for the monk. Commitment means we are going to show up tomorrow for work and will keep the same spouse we live with today. The more committed we are to our family, friends, and our convictions, the more free we become to be open to others. Commitment settles us down and makes room inside for another to enter. It resolves crucial decisions such as whom you will love and where you will live and what you will do with your life. By closing up some options, commitment frees you to live in peace with yourself. It quiets the struggles.

Over time, as our lives become more stable, we can begin to see the stranger less as a disruption and more as a gift. The stranger is a lot like God, after all. God is constantly disrupting our best plans; God shows up when it is less than convenient; God is present no matter what we do to shoo him off. How we live with all these strangers who keep messing up our plans will determine the future for all of us.

We don't have to have all the answers to companion the hurting. Actually, people who try to offer answers are not particularly comforting. Do we really think it would hurt less if we understood? Forget answers. Be available. Be available with eyes wide open. Know it is going to interrupt your well-planned life.

This kind of hospitality moves you past yourself, helps you to transcend yourself. To put aside my own pain and feel yours is truly a magical power. It is a power that can eventually transform the world into a place where no one is excluded and no tear goes uncomforted.

eleven

Calling a Truce—
Hospitality Toward God

few years ago a magazine editor asked me to write an article about doubt. We had worked together on countless projects. She knew me well, knew my abilities, my weaknesses, and she knew much of my story. Somehow, this knowing of me had convinced her that I was the right person to write an article about how faith crushes doubt. She was not prepared for the article I submitted, which suggested that doubt is an integral part of faith, not something to be avoided or denied, but a thing to be explored and embraced. Doubt is part of the gift we call faith, I concluded. My editor was aghast.

She scolded me for believing that doubt is God-given. Doubt is the enemy, she insisted, and is to be overcome, not embraced. There is no lesson to be learned in doubt, only a victory to be won. It is not our place to question the goodness of God; such a thing decreases rather than builds faith.

It was a stinging rebuke. The intensity of her reaction indicated to me that the topic was volatile and very personal for her. The right thing to do was honor this woman I liked and respected. By mutual agreement, we cancelled the project after she saw my first set of notes.

During that time, I did a lot of considering of my doubts. I admit that I am predisposed to doubt. I once heard Frederick Buechner say, "Whether your faith is that there is a God or that there is not a God, if you don't have doubts, you are either kidding yourself or asleep. Doubt is the ants in the pants of faith. They keep it awake and moving."

There is a kind of doubt that is unique to believers. It does the good work of keeping faith awake and moving. I am strongly inclined to that kind of doubt, the doubt that is born in a passion to believe. I think this is what I failed to communicate to my editor friend, that my own doubts have emerged from faith, not disbelief. I want, I need, I crave to believe more and more.

But sometimes life, and the way of the world, throws massive obstacles into the path of faith. It is no good to tell myself that God moves in mysterious ways. God could stop doing that. Being God does not necessitate the mystery and confusion, does it? Step out from behind the curtain, or risk appearing to be the odd, selfish little wizard from Oz.

Thinking people have issues with the way God runs the universe. Since God made people to think, we have to conclude that we are intended to ask the questions. Why does the person who voices doubt receive an onslaught of rebuke double-charged with guilt? If I can conceive the question, it merits asking regardless of whom it offends. God is not offended by my doubt. God's wide shoulders can handle anything I can dish up.

Here's what I know. If I had it within my power to keep people from suffering with cancer, I would. If I could protect every child in the universe from abuse and neglect, I would. If I could feed every hungry person, bring justice to every injustice, I would. If my best friend had a brother she adored who was dying and suffering, and she asked me to heal him—if I had the power to do so, I would. No questions asked. No questions needed. I would do it because I love my friend. I would do it because it's right. I would do it because cancer is a horrific disease. I would do it because I care—I care deeply.

Based on God's track record it appears that I am more loving than God.

While you may huff and puff that I think such a thing, you too have had moments when you wonder what the heck God is thinking. I doubt. And so do you. It's meaningless to say I believe if I have never doubted or questioned what I believe. It's not just meaningless, though; it's a lie. No such thing as belief can exist unless not believing is an ever-present option.

Doubt has at times driven a wedge in my relationship with God. I have walked away, or at least tried to walk away. This is what those who don't want me to talk about doubt fear most—that doubt will cause people to turn away from God. And yes, it just might. But faith that has never asked the difficult question isn't faith at all; it is merely comfort food.

The difference between doubting when your heart believes and doubt for the experience of doubt itself is that a believer's doubt does not lead to despair; it leads us back to God, deeper into God. Before that happens, it may strip us of all we ever believed about God, all our pet theologies and notions. Everything we learned in seminary or Bible school will fall by the way before doubt is finished with us.

We emerge from the dark night of doubt battered, but clear-headed. There is not much about theology that I can state without hesitation. I know the creeds, I have studied theology, but mostly when it comes to stating a theological matter I feel like I'm tossing darts at Jell-O. But I can state clearly what I have gained by doubting. Hope.

Faith is a gift of God, a thing that overshadows us and chases us down. We do not find faith; it finds us. Hope is a choice to believe, despite evidence to the contrary, that God is going to make sense of all this insanity someday. Healing will come in the wings of God, peace will cover the earth from shore to shore, and a thing so bright and beautiful will emerge that it will all have been worth it.

Faith crushes me sometimes, because I have found God to be maddening and inescapable. Hope is my response to this Divine Passion that chases me down when I run. Hope is the title of the truce between God and me.

It is hard to be accepting of God and God's way. Christianity has developed an entire language for our attempts. We say things like "Let God be God," and "God's will, nothing more, nothing less." All the while we fumble around wondering where God gets off to when God is most needed, and does God even see the little girl who will be raped by her father tonight? How about the couple who hope and pray for a child, finally adopt one after a decade of trying, failing, and anguishing, only to have that child killed by a falling boulder that crushes the little one dead in her baby seat—while they are on vacation? Make sense of that if you can, but don't dare suggest they should let God capriciously just be God.

Our attempts to explain God tend to the ridiculous. We dare to speak knowingly of God's will, and in the same breath speak of God as the great unknowable mystery who is beyond explaining. Our explaining of God eventually settles on the reality that God is not explainable. Perhaps the most honest thing we can do is throw up our hands and admit we haven't a clue what God is doing. If we are to let God be God, let's start with ceasing to defend or explain God. We are never more absurd than when we try to explain God.

I have had to forgive God for being obscure and magnificently mystifying. I've come to realize that God is not intentionally baffling; it is not some part of the bigger plan that we find God inexplicable. There's no big lesson in this state of God's being. It is just the state of what is. All that godliness makes God completely other, completely unlike anything or anyone else, and beyond comprehension. In the twisting turns of my journey, I've learned that it is my ideas about God that need forgiving—my idea that God would protect me, God would heal people I love, God would grant me and mine special benefits, God would right the wrongs.

God is not an insurance policy. God is not a benefit package. You can take God as is, or you can ignore God. The minute you begin to morph God into something tamer, you end up with less than God. You end up with an alter-ego. It takes great faith to look squarely at the state of what is and still trust in the goodness of God.

I believe God is good. I do not understand the goodness, though. I believe God loves, but it is a loving that in no way resembles my knowledge of loving. I cannot bring my knowledge or experience to the question of God and make sense of it. I hope in

God's love. I hope in God's goodness. I don't always comprehend the movements and presence of these realities in time and space, where I live.

Hospitality toward God has not come easy to me. But to be in relationship with God, which is inexorable, I have had to make peace with God on the only terms that make any sense. Hope. I have lost all my ideas about God, but I hope in God more profoundly than ever before.

God will remain mystifying and spellbinding. God may capture me completely and forever hold me ensnared to the beauty and wonder, while simultaneously allowing me a full view of the tortured and lost. If I am to love God, I must accept this as part of the deal. I am not allowed rose-colored glasses, pretty theologies, and whimsical beliefs about the will of God.

God, like any of us, insists upon being accepted as is, even with the maddening obscurity, dark night of the soul, and rocks falling on innocent babies. Take it or leave it, but don't paint it into a pretty picture, because it is anything but.

Welcoming God into my life is a daily exercise in faith and hope. When I extend hospitality to this baffling, enticing God, I also open myself to love the unlovable. To love God is to love the wild wind, the shaker of the universe, the fury of the stars, the broken child, the tortured captive; it is to find God where we don't want to look and to walk where even devils flee. Can we really look up at the crossed beams on Good Friday and think otherwise?

As Christians, this is the God we receive. The bleeding one, misunderstood, judged, put to annihilation for nothing less than the truth. Like the long-ago disciples, we still look for the conquering God who sets up a kingdom among us. What we find is the God who suffers at our hands. Suffering may never make sense, but God is not indifferent. Christianity tells us that we do not suffer alone—God is present in our bleeding, aching, throbbing. We are not abandoned. Not forgotten. We are carved in the palm of God's hand. We are unforgettable.

When God stands stripped of all the pretensions and misconceptions, all the silly and awful theology, I have discovered a God I can joyfully welcome even though God is pure and absolute Stranger to me. My attempts at hospitality are pretense until I have made peace with God and am able to honestly extend hospitality to the Divine who simultaneously bewilders and beguiles.

twelve

Listening—The Deep Truth of Hospitality

*L*isten to me!" This is the primal call of the human heart. There is nothing that characterizes the Benedictine life more than listening. It has been called the key to Benedict's entire spiritual teaching. More than anything else, a monk is called to be a listener. All of his days, the monk is trained to hear God. He learns to hear God in everything and everyone.

To Benedict, listening is not the same as intellectual comprehension. Listening, as Benedict understood it, is a special kind of deep attentiveness to all of life. Benedict understood that we can live in ways that either dull or sharpen this attentiveness. Benedict's Rule is a guide to sharpening the ears of the heart.

The place of listening in monasticism cannot be overemphasized. The monk who is not listening is missing the point. Kathleen Norris, author of *Cloister Walk*, tells a story about talking to one of her monk friends. They were in his office and she was trying to express something that mattered very much to her. But as she talked, she noticed he was preoccupied. After a few minutes of watching him be distracted and restless, she snapped at him, "Will you listen to me, please!" Listen. Ah. She had the Benedictine's attention. Listen, yes, that's what it is I'm supposed to be doing.

Many years ago my husband, David, and I lived across the street from a little log cabin. The place was abandoned and in rather rough shape. One autumn, a man moved into the cabin. David, being the outgoing type he is, went over and introduced himself. And being the introvert I am, I did not. Upon his return from the first visit with our new neighbor, Les, David reported that Les was going to fix up the place and sell it.

Not a bad idea to get rid of an eye sore. I didn't think much more about Les until a few nights later when screaming suddenly cut through the peace of the neighborhood. Horrible screaming, the kind that drives you into a fetal position if you hear it for too long. I went to a bedroom window that was opened just a bit. The screams were coming from the little log house. They were not actually all that loud—loud enough to hear, but not ear-piercing. It was the suffering that was so loud. They were the screams of a grown man. The next night, I woke up to his screams again. And the next. Then silence for several nights before the screams happened again.

The screams haunted me. I made a plan. On a cool autumn day I took a bowl of chili and a thermos of coffee and some apple cake to Les. I introduced myself. It was not comfortable for either of us. He was a soft-spoken man who looked a bit like Willie Nelson with less hair. I didn't ask him about the screaming and he didn't bring up the subject either.

He talked about a marriage that failed and said he would never marry again. He said he had fixed up quite a few old houses. He lived in them, repaired them, sold them to "nice young families for a good price," and then he moved on. And finally, as he drained the last of the coffee he talked of Vietnam. He said, "I'll never get out of those fields." Les never said the words, but he asked me to understand his screaming. He asked me to give him a chance to repair the house and move a nice family into it. He asked me to be the kind of neighbor who will smile at you in the morning after you have spent the night screaming against the dark. He took a chance by telling his story and asking me to accept him and live for a season with his suffering. But he never said any of that.

Winter shut the windows and the drapes in the quiet neighborhood. I didn't hear his screams as often, but when insomnia hit, I would sometimes hear something coming from the locked windows across the narrow gravel street and I would pray for the man who could never stay in one place, because he could never forget another place.

Everything changes when you hear the screams in the night. You can't be the same after that—and if that doesn't make you cross the street with a bowl of chili and a heart ready to listen, nothing will.

When we learn to listen, we will hear screams, and the sound of another's suffering changes everything. It unsettles us, breaks apart our comfort, and makes us choose a side. We become less human when we decide to do nothing once we have heard the screams. Years of ignoring the pain around us makes us less able to respond. This is one way we become hard and closed. It isn't easy to stay open. God knows it isn't easy.

You can go along day after day, hour after hour, without hearing much of anything and then something slams into you and gets your attention. Some equivalent of a scream in the night. You didn't expect it, sure didn't want it, but it strikes you with such power when your guard is down that you end up listening, despite not wanting to hear another's pain.

One day when Father Dan was visiting his mother in a nursing home, one of the physical therapists taking care of his mother commented that she seemed rather depressed that day. His mother sighed and said, "Who the hell wouldn't be depressed?" She was right. You can't live sanely in this world without a heart that is breaking for yourself, and all of us, in this whole big mess. We are all lost together. We choose our own destruction rather than life. We know this is the truth and who the hell wouldn't be depressed about it?

You know it's true because every now and then you've listened enough to hear the truth. You have seen more than you've let on. Through moments of blinding beauty and deafening pain you have heard the *more* that runs through it all.

Benedict calls us to hear the *more*. Listen, the ancient monk tells us, listen. It will break your heart, but it will also give you a heart. And it will give you more—it will give you life. Only love is strong enough to hold all the pain in the world. Love will listen. If you aren't listening, you aren't loving.

Listening is always involved in hospitality. The most gracious attempts we can muster are meaningless if we do not actually hear the stranger. Listening is the core meaning of hospitality. It is something we can give anyone and everyone, including ourselves. It takes only a few minutes to really listen.

A young man who worked all during his high school years bagging groceries said that the vast majority of people who went through his line never looked at him when he asked, "Paper or plastic?" He said people did not meet his eyes, smile at him, or acknowledge him in any way. What a tiny thing. Look up; look into the eyes of the young person and smile.

The former bagboy said, "My mother asked me one day why I always hung around her, talking, after work. I didn't know why until Mom and I talked about how I feel at work. I feel like I'm not quite human."

This is what happens to the one who feels as if no one ever listens. Most of us cannot imagine such an existence, but there are homes and places where people are not heard. Children are often not listened to; they are viewed as objects to be maintained rather than real human beings.

A young couple was in a restaurant with their four-year-old son. They were being waited on by one of those experienced waitresses who never show contempt for a customer, but by their unhurried pace and level gaze make it evident they fear no mortal, not even parents. She jotted on her pad, deliberately and quietly, while the parents gave their selections, including substitutions and such. She turned to the boy and he began his order in a kind of fearful desperation.

"I want a hot dog," he started. His parents barked in unison, "No hot dog!" The mother scowled at the boy, who fell silent, and said, "Bring him the vegetable and grilled chicken, milk and . . ."

The waitress ignored the parents as she looked directly at the boy. "What do you want on your hot dog?"

The amazed child said, "Lots of ketchup, and a pickle, too. And could you bring some milk?"

"Coming up," she said and turned from the table, never even looking at the stunned parents. The boy watched her depart with astonished delight and then said to his dismayed parents, "You know what? She thinks I'm real! She thinks I'm real!"

That's how you feel when someone listens to you: Real.

Every person is born with the right to become exactly who they were created to be. When a human being isn't heard, when all that is special to a child is ignored so that the child can be shaped into what the parents think the child should be—that person is in grave danger of becoming less than they were made for.

Hospitality is a way to counter the thousands of times another human being has felt less than human because others didn't listen. Listening is the power of hospitality; it is what makes hospitality the life-giving thing it is. When you listen, you get past yourself too. That is something we all need to do a little more. In the listening stance, the focus switches from the self to the other.

Every now and then we meet someone who is very good at listening. When people have been with someone who really listens, they feel better about themselves. "I feel like someone is listening to me for the first time," a number of people have said about their association with the monks of St. Benedict Monastery. There is nothing more human than our desire to be heard. It is our cry for permission to live.

The woman in the grocery store who talks about how her toddler isn't potty-trained yet. The old man who talks about how often it has snowed in March since 1941. The man who tells the same old joke every time you see him. The woman who never ceases discussing her health problems. What all of these people have in common is that they are looking for someone to affirm them and give them permission to be.

There is so much in life that is potentially dehumanizing. Listening is the most hospitable thing we can do, and if we do no other thing than train ourselves to listen to others, we will have taken great steps in hospitality.

One of the local discount stores in our area makes a practice of hiring many disabled persons. Some of them are physically disabled, others are mentally disabled. These special employees tend to be given the task of putting your new sweatshirt, socks, and cabbage into bags. Watch the people in those lines. Some of them are actually pretty comfortable with the interesting and different people at the end of the line waiting to bag their underwear. Others do everything they can to ignore these people.

Imagine you are in line behind a very nice woman who is clearly uneasy with the young man bagging her purchases. It happened to a friend the other day.

The guy bagging was probably thirty-five, but mentally closer to twelve or thirteen. He was blonde and short with a wide smile. He had a scar across the left temple that was at least three inches long. He probably had not been born with his disability. He wore a name badge that read, "Kevin."

Kevin greeted the woman and said, "Are you in a hurry today?"

She did not look at Kevin. She looked at the woman ringing up her order and managed a faint smile. She said, "The lines are rather long this morning." The woman nodded and kept dashing things through the scanner.

Kevin tried again, "You have a lot of pop here. Are you going to have company?"

The older woman turned toward the person behind her in line, as if looking for help; she had a frantic look in her eye. She was not a mean-spirited woman; she simply had come of age in an era when such a young man would have been institutionalized, rather than commenting on her purchases.

The woman behind her, my friend, smiled and said, "You do have a lot of pop."

"My grandson is turning fourteen. It's for his party."

"My sister had a birthday party," the disabled young man said. He drooled and it landed on a liter-size bottle of green pop and rolled off. The woman at the register glanced from the drool to the boy and kept working.

"I'll bet that was a lot of fun," said my friend.

Then the woman buying pop for her grandson's party did a courageous thing. It was so brave you wanted to cry for her. She turned toward Kevin, took a breath, and looked him in the eye. She said, "Did you enjoy the party?"

Kevin nodded. "I like parties. My sister says she gets two birthdays a year because I'm such a pain in the butt, so she gets mine." He grinned. "But she don't mean it because she always takes me to the show for my birthday and I get the biggest bag of popcorn." He looked up from his bagging and said, "I love my sister."

The woman blinked back tears. Kevin was only twelve inches from her and he was a real live human being now, and she didn't even want to escape him any longer. She touched his hand and said, "I am certain that she loves you, too."

"Yup, that's why I get the biggest bag of popcorn," he said.

Right there in the checkout line, day after day, are encounters between people like the old woman and Kevin. Sure, you know there is some politically correct employment policy behind the employment of the special people stuffing bags at this discount store, but so what? The result is magic: humans understanding other humans a little better.

Kevin probably gets ignored often, but you know Kevin is used to it. Now that he's out there at the cash register, every now and then someone will look Kevin in the eye and they will affirm him, they will grin at him, they will listen to him. And that would not happen without that politically correct employment policy.

It is very good for Kevin, but if you have known a few people like him you know that he will be okay anyway. There is an ability to love, understand, forgive, and accept in the Kevins of our world that is beyond understanding.

The one who otherwise would have avoided Kevin is the one who is really changed when he first listens, when he first discovers he can no longer ignore someone whose only crime is making him uneasy. Listening is the core of hospitality, and while the people we listen to benefit, in the end we are the ones transformed.

Benedict doesn't call us to listen on the surface. He wants us to listen with the ears of the soul. Listen way down deep. You know the place; it's the same place that weeps at the sight of a newborn, the same place that falls silent at the edge of a mountain, the same place that reaches for a falling sparrow. Listen from *that* place.

Listening is a choice to be receptive, to stop speaking and take an open stance. It involves patiently waiting for the real self to be revealed, even if just a little bit of the real self. Listening means we move past what we think we know, and by listening to someone else's story, we learn something we would not have discovered any other way.

Listening is important because it forms bonds between people and reinforces self-worth. People feel better when they have been listened to. Listening helps us understand how others are different from us, and how they are the same. By really hearing someone, we come to realize that we never perfectly understand anyone. That realization helps us drop the unrealistic expectation that anyone will ever completely understand us. Listening validates the one you listen to; it affirms him and reminds him of his basic worth.

A friend tells the story of his son Paul who was, at the age of eleven, taken to meet his great aunt in a nursing home, where she had been moved from out of state. Aunt Margaret was in the advanced stages of dementia. She was, however, thrilled to see Paul. She touched his face and stroked his hair and held his hands while she told him stories of eighty-five years ago, stories of being a girl almost a century ago.

As she talked and talked, the father grew concerned that his son's lesson in respect and kindness was going to be ruined by her endless "when I was a girl" chattering. He interrupted with an excuse and got Paul out of there. On the way to the car he tried to explain dementia to his son. Paul stopped him and said, "Hey, Dad, you don't have to make excuses for Aunt Margaret. She was just remembering who she is."

Listening is at the heart of Benedictine spirituality because it is the only way to see through the eyes of another. When we listen to another, we catch a slight glimpse of their soul. We create an open page where they are free to write their story. We help people remember who they are.

Another friend told me about the day her husband called to tell her he wanted to bring home a guest, a woman from South Africa. She told him no, don't even think about it, buster. It could not have been a worse day, she explained.

The washing machine had busted and she was out of diapers, so the babies had dishtowels pinned to their bottoms (they were the parents of boys, two sets of twins, aged two and five). There were no clean towels and the beds were stripped and all she had were soggy sheets. She explained that she planned to serve boxed macaroni and cheese and hot dogs on paper plates for dinner. She told him that she had not had time for a shower and did not see any break in her schedule for that particular luxury before midnight.

What's more, when the dishtowels on the babies' bottoms became soiled she would be stripping them down to naked.

"'No,' I told him, 'do not bring this woman home, not today.' He begged. He said we were exactly what she wanted to see, a normal American family. I pointed out that not many American families had a lunatic for a mother, and two sets of twins, and he just laughed. He said she would love hot dogs and the twins and the paper plates and even little lunatic me. I gave in."

That night over paper plates and boxed macaroni the woman, her husband, and their four sons heard the stories of apartheid. The mother knew the youngest two would not remember them, but she determined, before the meal was over, she would tell the stories to her sons again and again. She would not let them forget. The guest had once had her own sons, two of them. They had both been killed in the violence.

The guest helped clean up, she helped put the children to bed, and then she sat on their front porch steps and cried while she smoked one cigarette after another.

"She was a child of God who had lost her way," my friend said. "She didn't know if she would ever go home again. She told me weeks later, she opened her heart to a white woman for the first time in years. She wasn't the only one who was changed that night, though. I learned the stranger comes to me with the message of an angel, a gift to give me that will change my life."

Hospitality is a way to take the gift of life seriously. We hear a great deal of talk about the sanctity of life, but we see few people living in a way that celebrates it. By our best and worst attempts at hospitality we say to ourselves and to the whole world:

Everything matters.
You are not alone.
You are more than you know.
The awful thing is not the final word.
Today is all we have and today is enough.
We need each other.

On one of my first visits to help with the teen retreats at the monastery, I met a teen girl who had just been through the death of a friend. She was not a participant of the retreat; she just showed up on Saturday morning because she needed to be with friends to grieve.

Father Dan knew the girl; he also had known and loved the girl who died. The retreat house was jammed with teens. In addition, more adults had accompanied the youth than usual. It was crowded and they had a schedule to keep, goals to accomplish, youth to guide and help.

What amazed me that weekend was not the way the staff made all the teens feel special, even though they did. What amazed me was how tenderly Dan stood beside one teenager who was having a tough time. And she was not a retreat kid. She was a drop-in. But that was okay. Sometimes you need to be where you'll be understood.

I didn't witness many conversations between the two of them. What I saw was Father Dan listening to someone's grief in a profound, but subtle, way. The monk was present to the girl in small ways, sitting with her, hanging up her coat, pouring her Pepsi, touching her hand at just the right moment. It was not some skill he had learned; it was just who he is, who he has become through the years of following the Benedictine path.

Becoming a person of hospitality is not just a matter of learning Benedictine ideas and then applying those ideas. That's a pretty good place to start, but truly learning them takes a lifetime. You will not even know when it happens—that is how natural being hospitable will eventually seem.

During a three-city book tour I had the chance to recognize just how far I have to go before becoming as hospitable as Father Dan. We were on the third city of the tour. We were exhausted and crabby and our usually friendly conversation had turned a bit surly. We were close to collapse from exhaustion. A center for retired Benedictine nuns had invited us for a visit on Sunday. Dan gave the homily at mass, after which we had breakfast with some of the sisters. I ate my eggs, hoping for a nap as soon as we could get back to our hotel.

But a nap was not in my near future. Instead, I found myself on a tour with some of the relentlessly cheery staff, also Benedictine nuns, who wanted to introduce us to each and every nun in the whole place. Every nun, in every bed, in every room. This did not improve my attitude, I promise you. I was pretty locked up inside myself, not paying much attention to the sisters, as we moved from room to room.

I'm not sure which sister got my attention, but in the course of our introductions one of the nuns reached out and took Dan's hand and took mine. I was jerked back from the selfish depths of myself long enough to notice that Father Dan was connecting—I mean intentionally pushing past his exhaustion to connect with every single person he met. He asked questions and sincerely listened to them. He laughed with them, he touched them. Even in fatigue he was present.

There was some deep well, some resource, he was drawing from, a place I had not yet discovered in myself. It reminded me of the story of Jesus meeting the woman at the well. Tired, hungry, and weary—that is what the Savior of the World was that day. He was in a place nice Jewish boys did not go, talking to the kind of woman Mary probably would have told him to avoid. It is one of the liveliest conversations recorded in the Gospels. They banter, they engage, they chide, and they connect. The Lord of the Universe is enjoying himself because he's got a live one.

Jesus hears her, really hears her, in a way no other person has ever heard her. She tells other people that he has understood her in a way no other person ever understood her. It is such a remarkable thing for her and it costs this dear Jesus so much. His followers return and urge him to eat, to keep up his strength. He tells them that he is fed from a place they do not understand.

That day watching Father Dan, an ordinary tired and grumpy guy who is also a monk, I wondered if I could ever do what he was doing. I hoped, fiercely hoped, that someday I would. I told him how impressed I was with what I'd seen him do, and he gave me this weird look and changed the subject. It came so naturally to him that he was not aware of what a remarkable thing he did.

You have probably heard news stories about the brilliant inventor Dean Kamen. He has invented, for example, a wheelchair that can navigate stairs without any special equipment. The same wheelchair also allows the person sitting in it to raise the seat so that he or she can look other people in the eye. Sounds like a pretty amazing piece of equipment, doesn't it?

We can do even more amazing and profound things for one another. Nothing will keep the pain from crippling each one of us from time to time. We cannot escape that reality. But we can help each other climb the difficult stairs of our lives; we can help each other when moving under our own steam just is not going to happen. We can raise each other up in dignity, and look right into one another's eyes. We can help each other make it to places that have been closed to us.

One of the most memorable lessons in listening to one another happened during my days of sitting in a hospital waiting room. I invite you to go back all those years and join us.

When my infant daughter was being treated for cancer we spent a lot of time in a waiting room on the seventh floor of Children's Hospital in Detroit. The babies and toddlers, the kids and the teens, all waited in that room for a turn at having chemicals put into a vein in the desperate hope of stopping cancer in its tracks. Parents, relatives, and friends waited with the children.

I was there with my little baby; often my father was with me. It's not spoken, but we had something like assigned seats in that place and somehow we all found out one another's story. I don't recall much talking about cancer, but we heard each other in other ways—ways I don't remember anymore.

On this particular day one of the chairs is empty, and we all know what that means. It means one of us isn't coming back. One of us is gone. Another one has lost. That makes the waiting room quiet.

I'm not the only young mother in the room. There's one next to me with her son Matthew. Matthew is a year old. He's very thin with sticks for arms and legs. He has the largest eyes you will ever see on a child. He's bald. Most of the kids are bald. Chemo.

Across from Matthew is a teenaged girl, probably fourteen or fifteen. She, too, wears a stocking cap. Matthew's is red; hers is navy blue.

The girl has been there since before Angie and I started in the waiting room. She's curled up in her chair in something like a fetal position. In any other place on the planet, people would be very concerned about what she is doing and how she looks. Here—well, here nothing is like anywhere else on the planet. She is with her aunt because her single father won't go to the hospital with her. It is too hard for him to bear, he says.

Matthew's mother puts him on the floor. Show time. He pulls himself up to standing, using one of the orange plastic chairs to balance, and then he lets go and just stands there wobbling. He has our attention. When a child like Matthew does something as ordinary as take his first steps, it is good news in a place like this, a sign of hope. We cling to every crumb of hope.

The girl is watching. She doesn't want you to notice, but she's untangled those long, skinny arms and legs of hers and is slouched in the chair now, peering at wobbling Matthew from under her stocking cap. Matthew's sky blue gaze fixes on the girl. He waves his arms and he's off—walking, really walking—while his mother beams at this never-before-seen event.

He takes seven steps to the girl. I count them. He bumps into her bony knees, slaps his hands down on her legs, and looks up at her with a great big grin and grunt of triumph. Magic. Her face is changing, transforming into a smile that reaches her young eyes and makes her pretty again. She speaks.

Another first. "Can I hold him?" she asks the mother. "Sure." She scoops up the baby into her arms, "Well, Mr. Matthew, aren't you something!" she says softly and snuggles him tight to her caved-in chest. He relaxes against her, tucks his head under her chin, and spreads his arms wide open around her shoulders. He takes a deep breath and exhales. He goes limp. They sit there like that, the two of them. It's hard to tell who is holding who.

They have found their way home to each other. They have heard each other when no one said a word. Their connection is the same one we all share—our frail humanity. We do so need each other, and doesn't it terrify us?

With all its unforgettable beauty, this is still a sometimes dark and sometimes shuddering world we live in. We recognize this, no more profoundly than when we discuss such things as children living and dying with cancer, or the horrors of terrorism. It is a courageous thing to keep getting up every day, and it is a much more courageous thing to rouse your heart and incline it to love. To care for each other, to open the door to the stranger, to open your heart to the stranger, lifts you up into the great dance of life.

There is a wider way, a higher way. To go this way we must keep our hearts open to the possibility of serendipity in the eyes of the stranger.

God is among us. In a world where we see only in part and know even less, it is hard to spot God. Our eyes are not trained to see any better than our ears are trained to listen. It is not important that we recognize God in the stranger; God is there whether we notice or not. We can just assume that fact and do the next thing—accept the stranger.

What matters is that we stretch our hearts open and draw near to each other. It is the way of hospitality, the way of life, and it is, in this remote place where we have awakened to find ourselves, the only way home.

A Radical Hospitality Congregation Plan

he phrase "radical hospitality" has become common since the original writing of this book nearly ten years ago. It's used a lot by churches and organizations desiring to articulate a vision of welcome and acceptance to those who don't attend their church.

Why did the concept of radical hospitality speak to so many people? My best guess derives from the readers I've met in my book travels. It seems that we want to be more radically hospitable to others because most of us wish we were more accepted. We don't expect people to always understand, but we are sick at heart wishing others would just take us as we are.

Those who value faith and spirituality are, more and more, finding themselves to be strangers in the land. The messages of faith seem irrelevant to the mainstream culture. As a community, those who care about faith are a voice in the wilderness.

We want a world, a community, a home, a life that welcomes us rather than indifferently shoving us to a corner, or using us to meet some agenda. We want it for ourselves and for those we love. Simultaneously, we recognize that we are sadly incompetent at being for others what we want most for ourselves.

Religious organizations are trying to be relevant in a very trying time. Programs are offered, services provided, felt needs considered. Yet, we know that what those visitors at the door really want is welcome and acceptance. One of the most important things we can do is to begin to view the stranger not in terms of what he wants from us, but as a bearer of gifts that will enrich us.

Will the stranger become less frightful if we can reposition our minds to think of guests as the bearers of gifts from the rich depth of their experience? If we can, as a faith community, change how we view the outsider, it is a fine beginning.

While the multitude of radical hospitality workshops, conferences, study guides, and small groups has been exciting to observe and be a part of, it's also somewhat disturbing when a concept intended to change the human heart is reduced to a few steps or a program. This book was consciously written to incite thought, reflection, and maybe a conversion or "aha" moment now and then.

Sure, it's possible to create a list of how to become radically hospitable. It's been done. However, it was never the purpose of the first edition of this book. We made an intentional choice to avoid a "how-to" approach in the writing. Instead, we told stories, shared experiences and frustrations. The struggles of real people trying to get over themselves and open up a space inside for someone else—that was the story of the first edition. And it's still the message.

Radical Hospitality is not the blueprint to a program. This is not to say that it can't be used as a foundational approach to a program—many have done so. Programs and learning experiences are valuable. But spirituality is an inner work. As in the first edition, this book is occupied with becoming, rather than "how-to."

No program can replace the messy work of changing ourselves—of redemption and transformation. Much of what has gone wrong in our faith and intimate communities involves misguided attempts to simplify complex ideas, rather than allowing the human soul to expand, consider, deal with conflicts within and without. Growth happens no other way.

We can make ourselves available to learn and grow. But like the wildflowers, we are done to, something moves upon us, and we grow as we remain present to the possibility of transformation. We cannot make it happen. We must wait for the coming of the rains, the warming of the air, and the budding of the soul.

Changing the heart . . . it's a messy process and a painful one. Reconsidering a belief system long-held is worthwhile, but it is also excruciating. What we believe makes us who we are, as human beings. When we reconsider, abandon old ideas, move into new thinking or attempt a new perspective, we lose parts of ourselves. Maybe parts we're better without, but the amputation of a diseased part is still agonizing.

If we are serious about becoming more hospitable, we'll need something more powerful than a program to get where we're going. What this book does best, I think, is provide a companion. I've looked suspiciously at the stranger. I've crossed the street when I see someone I don't want to talk with. I've looked away from the sad eyes of a friend. I'm not proud of it. I know you aren't either. Through the processes of trying to be more accepting, I am constantly assaulted by how I remain insidiously unaccepting. For our journey, you and I need a guide.

Because many organizations have expressed an interest in programs and learning experiences related to radical hospitality, it seemed practical to offer some ideas for nurturing radical hospitality in the community setting. I hope these suggestions will make this book a useful guide for groups.

What, then, are the "steps" a group can take toward practicing radical hospitality? Looking again to St. Benedict for direction, the lessons come from monasticism.

An inner reality/awakening needs to happen first. As a group, as individuals, those who wish to make their community more open to others must become convinced that it is necessary. It's not just a good idea, not just a fine program, but a water and breath kind of necessity. When the concept is spoken of, studied, and planned there is a real danger of the whole process being unconvincing. People are not stupid and they don't want to be the victim of your well-meaning but heartless hospitality. Benedict warns his monks never to "feign affection"; the same goes for hospitality. Let whatever program you develop emerge from conviction.

Space and preparations are necessary. In the monastery beds are made, floors swept, windows washed, bathrooms scrubbed. The light bulbs are checked and a schedule of prayer, and possibly a map of the grounds, is put on a visitor's pillow. Towels are neatly stacked on a shelf. Windows are opened to let in fresh air. Your gathering space needs to be made ready. Make sure you have barrier-free entrances and exits. Does everyone have a song book they can read? Clean, dust, polish, put new books in the library, fresh sheets in the nursery, and fresh flowers at the door. Be sure the visitors' questions are answered. Provide someone of a similar age or demographic to companion the new person or family. Hospitality has always spoken to the practical. When coming in out of the rain, your visitors should not have to wonder what to do with their umbrellas. There is more involved in hospitality than training people to be nice and accept each other.

Be nice and accept each other. Many faith communities painfully function as a dysfunctional family. Personality disorders and complex personal relationships are just unavoidable. But if you want to welcome others, your group will have to get over it, get past it, and find ways to actively forgive and accept each other before ever being capable of truly welcoming others. Heal thyself. Hospitality isn't about what your group needs, or its mission statement, or meeting your objectives. It is about serving the guest. Genuine hospitality will cause your group to stretch beyond themselves, and this, too, is healing. Accept each other and your group will, inherently, become more accepting of others.

If you must draft a plan in a committee, remember that you are embarking on a journey to love and serve the stranger. Guard against the ease of developing a plan that will speak to your own needs and ambitions, rather than the welcome of your guests. Keep the reality of the difficult stranger ever before you. The one who makes you uneasy, the one you secretly wish would not go to your church. The one you avoid. Draft a plan to welcome *that* person and you might be on to something. But, hospitality is not an evangelism program, and any such attempt will be quickly recognized by your victims as phony and self seeking. Evangelism, disguised as hospitality, is certain to crash and burn at your feet. Pay close attention then: hospitality is not a church-growth program. It is our attempt to love "the least" among us, because in doing so, Jesus said we are loving him.

Hospitality does not encompass only how you greet people at the door, or how you follow up with visitors. That vision of hospitality is much too miniscule. Hospitality happens in the context of relationship, from the most casual to the most intimate. Build relationships by caring about what is happening to people. Several churches in my area bring a loaf of freshly baked bread to visitors within two weeks of their visit. It's such a lovely thing to do. But what if the guest needed the bread two weeks previously? Find out what people need and meet that need. A simple, polite set of questions beginning with, "Is there some way we can help you at this point in your life—right now?" would open the door. This can be accomplished by having a discretely different bulletin that is given to newcomers. Honor privacy and confidentiality, listen to people, and your group will become known as hospitable.

Have fun. Hospitality needs to involve people being together in fun, lively, energetic ways. Small towns and small congregations can often do this much better than larger ones. Host a picnic for the kids' baseball team at the end of the season, get the tweeners and teens together for a night of kickball by flashlight, pizza, and a movie. Hold potluck luncheons for your retired persons and then go bowling together. Don't always be serious; have fun. Look into one another's eyes and smile. These moments together build bonds and build community.

It's not a bad idea to have a Bible study or group lesson about hospitality, if your group responds to that sort of experience. This can be an opportunity to begin the process of internal reflection. There will be discussion in such a group, of course. Encourage people to move beyond how they felt when they first visited the church, or how it feels to be new in a group (unless someone has had a horrific experience at the hands of your group—that would have to be dealt with). You can be certain that all of us feel nervous and self-conscious in a new setting. Skip the obvious. Discussions are better directed toward topics such as: Who is missing from our group? Who makes me uncomfortable? Who would Jesus welcome? Who are we ignoring as a group? What bigotries do I clutch still? What can I do today to become more welcoming? Address the gut-level issues; get vulnerable and open. Then hospitality will emerge from the open places we create in our souls.

You can take all these steps toward hospitality, but if your heart isn't changed, nothing else will really change either. Don't be discouraged if your early attempts take your group back to the drawing board. View it as a process rather than an objective with a deadline. Becoming more open to others is always a process, whether for an individual or a group. Consider any setback an opportunity to learn more.

If early in this process your group makes strides in hospitality, don't rest in your good work. Continue to actively grow together in the process, to discuss what works and what doesn't. Once you have embarked on a journey toward hospitality, find ways to keep the discussion, and the transformation, alive.

Remember that you are embarking upon a conversion event. Benedictine monks speak of it as "conversion of life." It's actually a monastic vow. They vow before God that whatever happens today, they will show up tomorrow and try again. It is the work of a lifetime, but conversion happens day to day. Radical hospitality becomes a vibrant possibility in a community through the inner changes that happen individually. Let your efforts always strive to encourage hospitality and growth within the individuals who comprise the whole of your congregation. It is through our change of heart that we become more hospitable.

I would like to hear about your group's journey toward hospitality. Write me, in care of Paraclete Press, if you'd like to share your story:

Lonni Collins Pratt
Paraclete Press
P.O. Box 1568
Orleans, MA 02653

about paraclete press

Who We Are

Paraclete Press is a publisher of books, recordings, and DVDs on Christian spirituality. Our publishing represents a full expression of Christian belief and practice—from Catholic to Evangelical, from Protestant to Orthodox.

We are the publishing arm of the Community of Jesus, an ecumenical monastic community in the Benedictine tradition. As such, we are uniquely positioned in the marketplace without connection to a large corporation and with informal relationships to many branches and denominations of faith.

What We Are Doing

PARACLETE PRESS BOOKS | Paraclete publishes books that show the richness and depth of what it means to be Christian. Although Benedictine spirituality is at the heart of who we are and all that we do, we publish books that reflect the Christian experience across many cultures, time periods, and houses of worship. We publish books that nourish the vibrant life of the church and its people.

We have several different series, including the bestselling Paraclete Essentials and Paraclete Giants series of classic texts in contemporary English; Voices from the Monastery—men and women monastics writing about living a spiritual life today; our award-winning Paraclete Poetry series as well as the Mount Tabor Books on the arts; bestselling gift books for children on the occasions of baptism and first communion; and the Active Prayer Series that brings creativity and liveliness to any life of prayer.

MOUNT TABOR BOOKS | Paraclete's newest series, Mount Tabor Books, focuses on the arts and literature as well as liturgical worship and spirituality, and was created in conjunction with the Mount Tabor Ecumenical Centre for Art and Spirituality in Barga, Italy.

PARACLETE RECORDINGS | From Gregorian chant to contemporary American choral works, our recordings celebrate the best of sacred choral music composed through the centuries that create a space for heaven and earth to intersect. Paraclete Recordings is the record label representing the internationally acclaimed choir Gloriæ Dei Cantores, praised for their "rapt and fathomless spiritual intensity" by *American Record Guide*; the Gloriæ Dei Cantores Schola, specializing in the study and performance of Gregorian chant; and the other instrumental artists of the Gloriæ Dei Artes Foundation.

Paraclete Press is also privileged to be the exclusive North American distributor of the recordings of the Monastic Choir of St. Peter's Abbey in Solesmes, France, long considered to be a leading authority on Gregorian chant.

PARACLETE VIDEO | Our DVDs offer spiritual help, healing, and biblical guidance for a broad range of life issues including grief and loss, marriage, forgiveness, facing death, bullying, addictions, Alzheimer's, and spiritual formation.

learn more about us at our website: www.paracletepress.com, or call us toll-free at 1-800-451-5006.

SCAN
TO
READ
MORE

you may also be interested in

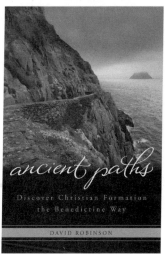

Ancient Paths
Discover Christian Formation
the Benedictine Way

By David Robinson

978-1-55725-773-4 Trade paper $19.99

Ancient Paths is a field-tested guidebook showing how "The Rule of St. Benedict," an ancient guidebook for Christian formation in community, has been lived daily by monastics over the past fifteen centuries. Through biblical principles and practical application, you will discover ancient but new ways of living your faith together with others. A twelve-week study guide is also provided for individuals, home groups, house churches, and small group leaders.

The Wisdom of Stability
Rooting Faith in a Mobile Culture
By Jonathan Wilson-Hartgrove Foreword by Kathleen Norris

978-1-55725-623-2   Trade paper $16.99

The Wisdom of Stability illuminates why staying in one place is both a virtue and good for you! When we cultivate an inner stability of heart—by rooting ourselves in the places where we live, by engaging the people we are with, and by observing the simple rhythms of tending to body and soul—true growth can happen.

The Rule of Saint Benedict
Paraclete Deluxe Essentials Edition

978-1-61261-769-5   Leatherette $17.99

A lovely leatherette keepsake edition of Jonathan Wilson-Hartgrove's vibrant paraphrase.

Available from most booksellers or through Paraclete Press:
www.paracletepress.com; 1-800-451-5006.